FROM THE

*H*EART

OF *P*EACE

Spriritual Teachings of
Baba Shivarudra Balayogi Maharaj

Shivabala – Shivarudra Bala Yogi Mission
Washington
U.S.A.

The material in this book was recorded, transcribed, edited, and proofread by devotees living in India, Australia, Singapore, Malaysia, Canada, and the United States. We wish to express love and gratitude to our Baba Shivarudra Balayogi, who is always speaking *From the Heart of Peace*.

Published by Charles and Carol Hopkins
P.O. Box 663, Hood River, Oregon, USA

First Edition..................................2007

ISBN 1-59975-866-0

Printed in India at
Shri Balaji Prakashan

I dedicate this book to the lotus feet of my beloved Master, the Divine Guru Shivabalayogi. He taught me, looked after me, brought me up—like a Mother, Father, Guru and God. Everything in this book that is good and beneficial to the humanity is His grace and blessings. Any short comings are mine. Every moment that I spent in His physical presence was a moment of leisure for me. Every moment He is with me to guide, to teach and to give experiences. He taught that those who can find their own faults and are ready to learn become great souls. He said ignorance is not a curse. Ego—not to learn, not be behave properly, not to consider about others, etc.—is the biggest curse. For me there is no difference between God and Shivabalayogi. May He grant refuge at His lotus feet and bless me to carry on His mission work.

Baba

Shri Shivabalayogi Mahraj

Note

The teachings transcribed in this book have been kept as close to Baba's exact words as possible. The feeling and strength of his verbal expressions have far greater value than conforming to rules of English grammar. These spiritual talks and answers to devotees' questions were complied between 2000 and 2005.

Baba teaches that God is that All-Pervading Omnipresent Supreme Being and can be worshipped in any form or formless. As his own beloved Guru and form of the Divine is Shri Shivabalayogi Maharaj, Baba may refer to the Divine in the masculine. God has no gender, but for the sake of teaching and understanding, these terms are used.

Forward

I met Baba's Guru, Shri Shivabalayogi Maharaj, who is known affectionately as Swamiji, in 1990 at the invitation of my friends Carol and Charlie Hopkins. My concern in meeting such a powerful Yogi was that he might want to control me or my mind. My friends reassured me that his teaching was about freedom and when I met him for myself, I experienced this to be true. I felt the great gift of his generous love. Meditating with Swamiji was an incredible experience; there was such profound silence and peace emanating from him as he sat, that my own meditation began to deepen. Being around Swamiji taught me the transformative power of being in the presence of an awakened soul. The core of his teaching is so simple— meditate and know your true Self. This realization of who you really are is the ultimate freedom.

Swamiji's most recent gift to us is his spiritual lineage holder, Shri Shivarudra Balayogi. Babaji, as he is affectionately known, is a profound and loving teacher whose Realization is very rare. Baba speaks English well, which Swamiji did not, so he is even more accessible to his western students' eager minds, though his message is still the simple and profound one that Swamiji brought—be still and know your true Self. Being in the presence of a true teacher such as Baba is a blessing—it is a rare opportunity to hear in words, and even more profoundly, in silence, the Truth of awareness. I am grateful to Swamiji and to Babaji for the incredible sacrifices they made to achieve Realization and for their generosity and love in offering their Realization freely, in support of freedom, to any who are interested.

Hood River, Oregon **Gretchen Lape**
January 2006

Shri Shivarudra Balayogi Maharaj

Introduction

"Surrender means letting go of mental agitation."

Baba

A true Yogi teaches primarily through silence. In the presence of Baba Shivarudra Balayogi, devotees often experience that the answers to their spiritual questions appear in their open hearts all at once—without any need of words. At that point, to continue asking the question is a joyful excuse to be there speaking with Baba. Being in his presence is like standing by the Gulf, looking into vastness. No words are needed and none can do justice to the experience of simply being—with the mind still and unobtrusive. To experience this silence, we need to be longing for it and receptive. As Baba says, "The mind needs to know that it is dreaming and that it must wake up." Many times over the years we have known Baba, we have seen how powerful is the silence that appears in, around, and as Shri Shivarudra Balayogi. We have experienced how devastating this silence can be to the imaginations and conclusions of a mind that has forgotten what underlies thought and belief.

A second way a Yogi teaches is by example. Baba is what he appears to be. He is kind, thoughtful and generous, but uncompromising when it comes to truth, and unbending with principle. A number of people have said to us, "Baba is the person I have always hoped to be." Before Baba began to teach Dhyana and Bhakti Marga, the spiritual paths of meditation and devotion, he

(11)

followed the meditation path to its fulfillment. He spent twenty years in service to his own Guru, Shri Shivabalayogi Maharaj—one of the greatest Yogic Masters of the twentieth century. Baba's request that we serve each other is supported by the fact that every day of his life is spent in this same service. Love in action is one form of devotion. Baba tells us that devotion, practiced with full attention, helps the mind focus on what is initially seen as "other", but in the end is revealed as the Self. Whatever your own outlook or spiritual ideal, you will find in Shivarudra Balayogi an example of that, in its highest form.

The third way the Yogi teaches is through words. Baba is a consummate communicator. Every answer he gives is simple, direct, and practical. He is not a preacher or a lecturer who must entertain an audience in order to keep them. The intention behind his words is not to bind but to help us stand on our own feet. As Baba has said, "I have learned from the Guru to walk without feet, to see without opening the eyes, to hear the truth without using the physical ears, to experience the truth without the ego of identification." The words of a Yogi come from and always lead back to the Heart of Peace.

Whether we are attracted to the Guru emotionally or because of the teachings, eventually our minds must go introverted to the Self. Baba teaches meditation because our minds have "gone out of control." His definition of meditation is: attention to. Meditation, over time and with persistence, allows the mind to subside and come back into the service of the Divine. In the privacy of our own being, we give our attention to the all-pervading consciousness that exists before thought, after thought, and in the gap between thoughts. The meditation technique Baba received from his Guru is ancient and effective. It allows us to come into intimate contact with the Ultimate Truth—the simple awareness of our own existence. In time all of us will "put the imaginations of the mind into the fire of the Self." Then, come what may, we are free. These are Baba's words; they come from direct experience. Baba is not simply passing on the wisdom of an ancient culture, as deep as that wisdom may be. He is revealing the truth that underlies all cultures and traditions. Baba's words are meant to help the devotee do what he has done. They undo the complex knots of the mind and allow what is simple to be clearly seen.

In some ways, talking with Baba is like talking with anyone else you love. Along with practical conversations about work in progress, there are weather reports, jokes, and occasional gossips. However, no matter what is being said, there is the awareness of Baba's words rising out of very deep water. We have come to notice and appreciate the seamless integration of deep silence with daily activity that Baba is bringing to the lives of his students. The Guru inspires by being a bridge between words, and that which is beyond the reach of words.

Clearing the doubts of devotees is one of the primary functions of the Guru. Baba has always been gracious to answer the sincere spiritual questions asked of him. Many people come to saints and Yogis for help with personal problems. We want health, money, relationships, and children. Baba reminds us over and over that Peace is the recommended goal. While he asks us to walk confidently toward this goal, he also teaches us that Peace is what we are; Peace is our own nature. What is needed is for the mind to settle, go inward, and become quiet. When the mind has given up all its roaming imaginations, we know that we are this Peace. There is nothing in the relative world that will satisfy the deep longing for the Self— beyond all experiences. With dedicated practice, determination and patience, this treasure, which is always present, will be revealed. Then the agonies of this world cannot bind us. How do we know that we are progressing? Baba says, "If your mind is becoming quieter, more still, then you are progressing."

We would like to thank all the devotees who have asked the questions that allow spiritual knowledge to flow from Baba. The deeper the question, the deeper the answer. We would like to thank those who have spent many hours transcribing Baba's talks, especially Jill Kieffer in Hood River, Oregon, along with Bruce and Anu Young in Perth, Australia. Thanks to Agastya Seward and Tabatha Wiggins for last minute proofreading and corrections. Many thanks to Clifford McGuire for the generous donation which made it possible to print this book. Thanks to Doris Brophy for loyal friendship and for her years of organizing public programs for Baba that gave rise to much of this material. Thanks to Rekha Sharma and Rahul Ghosh for organizing photographs, for grueling trips to the printer in New Delhi, and for taking good care of Baba. Finally, we'd like to offer gratitude and respect to General Hanut Singh, senior disciple of Shri Shivabalayogi Maharaj, for the steadfast kindness and encouragement he has given to Baba from Baba's early years in the Dehradun Ashram, continuing to this day.

All love, devotion and gratitude is offered to our dear Swamiji for training Baba to become the Heart of Peace.

Underwood, Washington   **Charlie and Carol Hopkins**

January 2006

THE GURU DISCIPLE RELATIONSHIP

Contents

PART TWO
TALKING WITH BABA

Answers to Spiritual Questions of Devotees and Sadhaks

PART ONE

SHORT TALKS BY BABA

Three Paths Of Sadhana

In the spiritual field, as in every field in the world these days, everyone is in a hurry to become gurus, instead of trying to learn things to achieve the Truth. We need a yearning to get to the Truth and adopt the right attitude. Very often when people get a little advanced in meditation, they can go into a blissful state. That can happen, but don't stop there. Peace is the recommended goal. When bliss occurs, the mind is likely to get excited. This can happen when you achieve something in the world also. You feel excited and blissful. This same blissfulness is misunderstood as the goal of meditation. But since ancient times, the Vedic Sages have recommended shanti (peace) as the goal. This is a natural peace in which the mind should be able to remain effortlessly.

It is not the mind's true nature to be wandering in the world like a monkey. The mind has lost its own real nature. Really we should use the mind and apply it on the brain to work in the world. Then, when your work is finished, the mind should go back to its origin and remain in peace. But it does not go back to its origin. It is in Viyoga, meaning: away from its origin. Yoga means reunion of the mind back to its origin. Viyoga is when the mind is distracted away from its original, true state. That is why the path of spirituality is also known as the path of Yoga, reunion.

Yoga Sadhana is a three fold path. First, we should look after the body by performing certain exercises and observing certain prescribed things to keep the body as healthy as possible. The body has to be naturally healthy. But the body does have limitations. It is not in our

(19)

hands to keep the body completely free of disease always. But, as far as possible, we shall try to keep the body healthy by doing exercise and looking after the food intake. The aim should be to generally not harm the body.

The next part of the path is with the mind. The mind is supposed to be at peace in the Self, just like the sun's rays in the sun or a droplet of the ocean, resting in the ocean. But the mind is out of control, it is in constant imaginations. It has gone into wrong habits. It has gone an unnatural way, Viyoga. This sadhana for the mind is the main section of Yoga on the spiritual path. We honor all the methods taught by the great Self-Realized masters of the world, which help you to control the mind, and help the mind recede to its original state. So many paths Shri Krishna taught in the Bhagavad-Gita. He taught Karma Sadhana, the path of service. "Live a worthy life," that is what He taught. Keep the mind in control under the original Yoga. Do your work simply as a duty, and then the mind won't get agitated with the work. Then you will find the mind doesn't brood or get anxious. If you are doing a duty, your mind is not supposed to go into agitation. It's your job. You simply do it. Just like when I am doing the mission work, I do it as a duty, not because I want fame or a large following. Whoever comes in front of me and is ready to listen to me, I will help them to practice, and guide them. Even if it were my own brother or sister, I would be teaching them the same way. There are no conditions, no demands, and no charge for my teaching. It can be anyone, a businessman, a student, anyone. All that is important is that you should have a yearning to know the spiritual truth. When you do work as a duty, it becomes Yoga Sadhana.

For twenty years in the ashram, every evening I did the bhajans and arati. It was my duty. I didn't bother how many people came. Whatever number came along, I did what I had to do. Whether twenty people came or two people came, or no people came. For many years, I had one mentally handicapped boy with me and I taught him to play and hold a particular note on the harmonium. Then I would play the dholak while I sang bhajans. For twenty years it was a sadhana, my duty. My God was there, my Guru was there. If my

Guru was there physically, I sang. If He wasn't there, I did it. I did my duty and did the sadhana. When I did this, the mind became peaceful. So all the work in life should be done like this; simply go ahead with the life you have chosen.

My Guru didn't prescribe sadhana other than to meditate, just one hour a day, and the rest of the time you just live your life. He said, "If you practice meditation, you will become better in all aspects of your life."

Bhakti Marga, the path of devotion, also has its own rules: surrender, devotion and faith. Every human mind has emotions, so if all the thousands of thoughts are trapped into one single thought, one emotion, one faith, then the mind becomes focused. We must live for what we believe and die for what we believe. We have one God, one Guru, and do not give up the faith, even if it means death. Never give up. Just like a tiger that would die of starvation rather than eat grass, we simply say, "We will do this," and then go ahead. I did this, and because of this, meditation was very easy for me; the mind had already learned to be quiet.

The third path is the moral Yoga Sadhana. My Guru used to say, "First become a better human being, then afterwards you can become an angel or god." We should be considerate to each other, forget and forgive. So many noble qualities exist. If we can behave like a perfect human being, that is Yoga Sadhana. Sometimes you might have heard people saying others are behaving like an animal. Instead of that, behave like a perfect human being. With meditation, it will be easier to do. If we are behaving in a natural way, that is Yoga. If we are behaving in an unnatural way, that is Viyoga. So adopt faith and inner strength and look ahead for the inner target. If we get distracted in meditation, with the mind thinking, 'What is happening?' again and again, then the mind gets distracted from the target. Then we get stuck in the path and we cannot progress in that path. So when we do things as a duty, then the mind settles. Even after my Tapas, I still follow this, just simply go ahead and do my duty, and do not worry about what others say. I just go ahead and do what I have to do for the Mission, as a duty.

God

Someone asked, "Can we see God if we meditate?" Yes we can. God is needed because you have imagined yourself as the droplet of the ocean, when you actually are the ocean. This is not something that can be explained, it has to be experienced. When we say, "see God," we don't mean through the physical eyes. God is not a physical entity in one place. Your mind is always imagining and in the process, it picturizes and visualizes all the time. Using that mind's technology, if the mind can be thinking of only one picture and if the mind becomes preoccupied with that picture, then the quality and potency of that picture becomes more and more strong within the mind. In the next stage, when you can raise the level of concentration and attention, then one will have visions based on that picturization. One will have visions of God. This is not an ordinary thing. In the third level, in Tapas, when the mind becomes 100- percent concentrated, then it touches the Self, like the sun's ray touching the sun. God manifests, but this is not final realization. For that the mind has to totally merge with the Self.

Think a little about God. If God is all-pervading, then there cannot be a thing which is different from God. So, through meditation, the mind—the droplet—becomes one with the ocean—the Real Self. In the beginning you shouldn't imagine that you are God. So when following the Bhakti Marga, the path of devotion, one starts out with dvaita, duality—the idea of you and your God as two separate things. I experienced this in my Tapas also. In the beginning you want something else; the drop wants the ocean. Gradually you begin to experience that you belong to God, until later finally you merge with it, and there is only ocean.

This is how I can say, "I love you all." Because I am able to see my own Self everywhere and because I see my Self everywhere, I cannot hate. I can only love. This is what is needed through meditation and if we understand this, then we can meditate properly. When we meditate we should simply watch and not get involved. If visions and thoughts come, then simply watch them, concentrate on them. They are a part of your Self. When speaking of non-duality, it is very often misunderstood. If you are going to live in this world, then you will have to play your role. But in time we need to rise above this duality of good and bad. The mind needs to rise above this duality. If God is in Rama, He is in Ravana also. So there should not be a misunderstanding in the name of non-duality. Common sense should be applied also.

It is like the story of the man who was in the path of the charging elephant. The elephant driver was calling out to him to get out of the way. But the man felt he was very wise and said, "God is in the elephant, so no harm will come to me." So he just stood there in the way of the charging animal. Then the elephant came and trampled over him and he was very badly injured. Later when he was on the bed, the people asked him, "Why didn't you get out of the way of the elephant when it was charging madly at you? The driver was telling you to move." The man simply replied, "I thought God was in the elephant so I would not be harmed." Then one of the other men said, "What a fool! If God was in the charging elephant, then He was also in the driver who was telling you to get out of the way!" So we have to use common sense also.

Humanity's Need For Prayer At This Time

Prayers made with total, unwavering faith will always be answered by the Divine Guru. We would call it a technological wonder. Mind—the conscious energy—is connected to the Divine, just like the sun's ray is connected to the sun. Due to distraction and constant craving of the mind, concentration and attention are severely affected. If you constantly practice meditation, in due course of time you can regain concentration. When the mind is totally concentrated, then it becomes capable of going introvert. Then if you pray, your Mind (Consciousness) can touch its origin—the Divine—and through an Automatic Divine Activity, the Divine's grace flows.

There are so many in this world who pray sincerely. For a while, though the situation may appear worse, by the grace of the Divine the situation comes back to peace. Look back into thousands of years of the history of the world; there always have been tension due to senseless behavior of humanity. Today there is an urgent need that we feel the responsibility to behave sensibly and maintain the dignity of humanity. This will be possible, only when we practice; possible when we practice austerities; possible when we practice meditation. Sincere meditation purifies the mind and its energies can then be programmed and channeled towards peaceful harmonious living. This is possible when we are ready to sacrifice selfish narrow-minded egotism.

Six Techniques For Surrender

Baba answers a devotee's question about surrender and mental agitation.

Devotee:

You said that the true definition of surrender was letting go of mental agitation. That is a very beautiful definition. I was wondering if you could help me to understand a little more deeply how that is done. I find sometimes that my mind gets agitated and it causes mental and physical tensions. Even if I have the intention of not getting agitated, at times I feel to be at the mercy of the mind. Can you help me to better understand how to let go of mental agitations and worries?

BABA:

1) Stick to the target and do not compromise. Never be satisfied with anything less than God, Self-Realization.

2) Always remember that finally everything is illusion. A thought of reality in the mind makes the mind feel agitated. Once the mind firmly realizes that nothing really exists and this is only a long dream and illusion, then things become trivial and agitation automatically goes away. For this purpose only, so that the mind surrenders, the Guru repeatedly teaches that everything except The Divine is unreal and illusion, both transitory and unreal, only a reflection of the mind.

3) When agitation occurs and you feel helpless, try to remember that the agitation also is unreal and transitory. When the mind is

firmly of the opinion that a particular thing is real, then mind enjoys getting into the imagination of agitations and so on. Seriously, the mind will believe anything as real and enjoy it.

4) You must know that as the mind enjoys the good, happiness and so on like positiveness, it also enjoys the bad, unhappiness and so on like all negativeness. This is the duality, taking the fuel of which, the mind is in wandering existence. This is also illusion. Everything the mind feels and experiences is simply its own imagination and thinking. The mind can never reflect the reality, the Ultimate Truth. When the mind stops, then existence is the Self and reality. A Yogi simply exists and does not think, "I am this or I am that." Nothing is real.

5) As you shall not analyze or judge anything, do not analyze or judge the agitation as agitation. Then it will stop. Nobody is having any agitation. Your Self is not having any agitation at all. There is no agitation at all. The Guru says, "Come on, get up! You are dreaming."

6) As long as the mind has the imagination that it is having fun, it holds on to the thought. Once the mind realizes there is no more fun in that imagination, it drops the thought, that which is giving trouble. It no more enjoys any agitation and drops it.

The Need For Faith And Devotion

To receive the grace you need to be receptive, and to become receptive we need to develop faith and devotion. My Guru used to say that the Guru's grace is always flowing, just like the wind is always blowing or the water in the river is always flowing. You need to build a dam to catch that grace, and that dam is made of faith and devotion.

Even since childhood this faith and devotion came very easily to me, very automatically. At one time when I was very young, I was very attracted to one particular saint, and I found a photo of him in a shop. I bought the photo and took it home and put it on the altar in the house. One relative of mine came later and ridiculed the photo being on the altar. He said that this man was not a saint. He had heard stories about him, and said that he was just a charlatan and not a real saint. When my mother heard these stories, she went to remove the picture from the altar, but I said, "No, do not remove the picture. The picture is my faith. If the saint is wrong, that is not my problem. Leave the picture itself, as it is my faith. Leave my faith intact." Subsequently, it was found out that the stories accusing the saint of wrong things were false, and he was revered widely as a great soul. The point is that it was about my faith, not the man himself.

Some people also just try to capitalize on shaking people's faith for their own advantage. Some years ago there was a politician in South India who started ridiculing about God, saying there was no God. Swamiji wrote a letter to him saying to him, "If you don't believe about God, then come to me, and I'll show you God." The politician wrote back to Swamiji, "We respect You very much, and we do believe in God. We just said this to get peoples' votes."

When I had faith, no power could affect it, no power could shake it. Even during my Tapas also, there was a test at the end. God came in front of me to test me. He said, "I have come to you because of your Tapas." Now when God comes in front of you, it is simply not possible to lie. Whatever is inside you will simply come out of your mouth as words. God was trying to create an ego, that it was my Tapas that had brought Him there. He said, "Now that I have come, you don't require your Guru anymore."

But the truth, which was inside me, simply came out of my lips, and I replied, "No, I want to be simply at the Lotus Feet of my Guru always." I felt it was Guru's grace that had brought God, not my Tapas. God then said, "The Guru will look after you and will guide the right devotees to come to you." I sometimes think, "Why do they come? Why do they love me, when I have nothing much to offer?" It is simply their love for me which brings them.

I saw Swamiji during His life on this earth never showing favors to people because of their status in this world. I saw Him going equally to palaces and small cottages, in big cars and small cars. It was the people's devotion which drew Him, not their wealth. He looked for the love.

Sometimes Swamiji would tell us, "If God gets angry with you, Guru will protect you. If you have faith in Guru's name, even God can't hurt you." Sometimes He would give a terrible scolding and the tone of His voice would go very high, then suddenly it would go down quickly and his voice would be back to normal. Then instantly He would say, "Now that I've tried to find fault with everything about you, you must want to go away from here, from this ashram. But I love you, and I simply wanted to remove some previous karma from you."

In the story of Rama and Hanuman, Rama wanted to murder Hanuman. That is the word used in the story, murder. But still Hanuman simply went on reciting Rama's name. He didn't bother him. Hanuman said, "Simply if my beloved Shri Rama wishes to kill this body, fine. No problems." He just went on reciting Rama's name.

Faith and devotion can see you through. When you listen to the Guru, have faith and devotion. Remember, "Seek and you shall find. Knock and the door will be opened unto you." If you meditate you will have a beautiful life in this world. It is difficult to live in this world. Remember bad karma will always come back on you. I have seen this so often in this life. People who have tried to cause problems to others, have always had it come back on them. If you have sincerity and faith, then you will get the Guru's blessing, God's grace. You will get peace and happiness and your mind will be controlled. Meditation will give you both knowledge and devotion. The path of devotion is also not easy. It needs one's complete attention. If you are devoted, your attention will always be on that form which you have chosen to be devoted to. Without devotion, you cannot have dedication. This meditation is like earning money for the mind. Meditation is like earning for the future. Swamiji did twenty hours or more per day of meditation during Tapas. Similarly, I did eighteen to twenty hours per day, also. You can just do one hour, and then you will be adding money to your account slowly. One Indian saint was talking of Ramana Maharshi. He said, "Ramana has banked 100 dollars, while I have banked thirty dollars, so you should at least bank five dollars."

I don't have to even come out of the ashram in Dehradun. There is everything I need there. But I'm aware of my Guru watching, so I do the work. Saint Kabir Das recites in one of his songs, "Puffed up, this mind has become puffed up and is wandering in this world like a drunken monkey. What a great magic that God has spelled." When the world gives you things, then the thing's relatives will also come and sit in the mind. These relatives are stress and unhappiness. When God gives, then the relatives who come are peace, happiness, concentration, and a pure heart. If your attention is to God, you will get peace. If your attention is to the world, you will get no peace.

Firm faith has always kept me on the right path. Even when I wanted to go to Swamiji's ashram, my Mother was very concerned to protect me. She would ask, "What if He is not a real Yogi? What if the atmosphere of the ashram is not conducive to you?" I simply replied, "It doesn't matter if He's a Yogi or not. It doesn't matter if He's a saint or not. All I know is that I love Him." So that faith never varied. I just loved Him, and went to Him. People questioning couldn't disturb me. When your faith is like this, then the grace will have to come to you.

Saint Kabir Das in another one of his songs sings:

Guru and Govinda (God) are standing in front of me. The mind is temporarily a bit confused; to whom should the first namaskar go? But then the mind becomes clear. I shall bow to the Guru first, because it is only through the Guru that I learned about God.

So Swamiji used to say, "If God is angry, Guru will protect you. If Guru is angry, no one can protect." If you have reverence then you will practice this meditation. Meditation is hard when you are not sincere, when you have no faith, no discipline, and no patience. If you have these things meditation is easy. So be like a soldier. He practices with his weapons even when the enemy is not there. Then when the enemy comes, he is prepared. If he waits for the enemy to come, and then starts practicing with the weapons, it will be too late. In the same way, if you meditate now, then when the world comes to trouble you, then you will be ready for it. The mind will not be disturbed. One of the great south Indian saints said, "Now, while your body is healthy, remember God. If you wait until your body is old, it will be too late." God has given us a beautiful gift of a human body. Let us not waste it.

Live As An Example Of What You Are

I have always thought, why can't humans learn to live for each other? They are always against each other. Swamiji used to tell me, "Live such a life, so it can be an example to your students in the future." Even when He initiated me into Sanyas, He didn't give me the ocher robes that are normally given. "No," He said, "behave in such a way that others say you are a monk." In Sanyas, one must physically, emotionally, and mentally surrender and leave everything to God. Similarly, with your own children, teach them by your own example. You should not show any rudeness, but simply a firm resolve. If they don't behave, then simply let them know firmly but politely that if they behave this way, then they won't get what they want from you. If you wish to teach, first live a good type of life, so that it is your teaching.

If you meditate, you will develop a more purified mind, and then automatically all the forgiveness, forbearance, understanding and love will come, as a pure heart develops. If the development of the mind is such, this can even occur instantly. King Janaka wanted to attain Self-Realization, but he wanted to attain it straight away. He made a condition that his teacher should be able to grant him Self-Realization in the time it takes to mount a horse. All the priests and scholars came and gave great, long discourses on the soul and God, but still Janaka didn't realize the Self. Finally Sage Astavakra came into the court. He had been born with a very deformed body. He couldn't walk properly, but had to roll. When they saw him coming into the hall, all the courtiers started laughing. Astavakra said to the king, "I thought these people were all wise, but they are all fools. They think this physical body is me, but I am not this body." So the king thought he must be a great teacher, and he asked, "Do you have Self-Realization?" The Saint replied, "Yes."

Janaka asked, "Can you give it to me also?" Again, Astavakra replied, "Yes. But for this you must come down from that throne, and you must do exactly as I say." In the Guru-disciple relationship, the right attitude in the disciple is very important and must be developed. One has to follow the teachings precisely. So the Sage said, "If you are ready to follow my commandments exactly, then I can give you Self-Realization. But you must give me your complete surrender. If you follow my commands, you will get Realization. If you don't follow, you won't get it."

The condition set by the king had been that he wanted to attain Self-Realization within the time it takes to mount a horse. So they went to the horse and the Saint got the king to prepare to mount. He said, "You must give me your complete attention and must do exactly as I say. Now mount the horse." So the king, paying his complete attention, started to mount the horse. As he swung his leg up over the top of the horse, Astavakra said, "Quiet!" Instantly the king went completely quiet—quiet physically as well as mentally. The instant his mind was quiet, he realized the Self. This was because of King Janaka's complete attention to what his Guru was saying. So his mind became completely quiet in that one instant, and the Self was revealed.

Swamiji used to say that if you have complete faith in the Guru and what the Guru says, then even the Guru can't stop you achieving, if he tests you. This happens finally on the day the commandments of the Guru penetrate fully and deeply. Sincerity, devotion, reverence, and efforts, the Guru really needs these from you. You need determination, dedication and patience. Be serious in your efforts. After all, it is all for you.

Some Of Swamiji's Teachings To Baba

Practice the meditation. Our job is to motivate. Practice brings more wealth than tons of theories. My Guru actually spoke very little, but he did answer good questions put to him. Once a boy said to him, "I want Self-Realization." Swamiji told him to go to a shoe shop, buy some shoes and hit his head with one shoe! "Are you ready to surrender?" asked Swamiji. "Are you prepared to stick it out, even if I yell at you and find fault with you? You must lose the ego!" He used to say, referring to Babaji, "Look at this boy. Even if I cut him into pieces and throw him into the river, he will get joined up and come back to me." He was tough outwardly, yet soft in his heart—uncompromising like a father yet caring and compassionate like a mother. He would yell at us ashram boys and tell us to get out of his room. Then in the next minute, forget all about it, so we would go straight back in his room again! He would give us sweets and he used to say things like, "If you can take my slaps, the world will not be able to hurt you," and, "Don't be in a hurry to be a Guru."

You need to have discipline. Make a timetable and never miss your meditation session. Make it a priority. Don't put it off in favor of other things. Don't say, "tomorrow," or "maybe after breakfast," or "I'm too busy." If you put it off for just one day, you'll lose the benefit of several days meditation. Never miss your meditation! Never miss it the way you wouldn't dream of missing your dinner! Keep the phone off the hook while you meditate. Be disciplined, then things will become easier. Keep busy, or keep meditating. Remember, an idle brain is the devil's workshop!

Swamiji used to say to keep smiling. When someone was unhappy He would ask, "Are you going to be hanged in the morning? No, so this is not so terrible." For thirty-three years he handled people's problems, distributed vibhuti, induced faith and devotion, helped people gain courage and inner strength. He told people, "Sit for one hour of meditation every day, the other twenty three hours are available to you; you'll be fresh. Do the meditation every day." In those days before email, so many devotees used to send letters to Swamiji asking for help with their problems. We took care that the letters were answered. I personally took care to answer them. "Have faith, it will be alright." That was what I wrote. Hundreds of people used to come up to Swamiji at the programs. He spoke about meditation, the need to meditate and the benefits of meditation.

Now I would like to clarify some things about my Guru and what he taught. He taught meditation and the Bhakti Marga, the path of devotion. Swamiji wanted music and bhajans to be performed and He encouraged food to be distributed by devotees free of charge. There is a bhava or particular feeling associated with the giving of food, because once food has been offered to the Divine it becomes prasadam—blessed and auspicious, holy and sacred. Eating blessed food together produces a feeling of oneness among the people. Humans all share the basic need for food.

People in the villages can't easily understand the knowledge and wisdom expressed in Indian philosophy, but they do understand spiritual power when they see it. This alone can motivate them to worship the Divine. Without such displays of Divine power, such people think they have the free will to do anything they want, to eat if they feel like eating, to do anything they please. So where is the power of God, they ask themselves. To counteract this mistaken thinking, Swamiji went into samadhi in front of them and many of those who saw it went into a state known as bhava samadhi, for which there is no exact English translation, although the word "trance" comes closest to the meaning. Bhava means the mind's feelings focused to such a single-pointed intensity. For example, suppose you get attached to one particular form of God or a particular Guru. The mind gets absorbed in the Divine and you might get visions, or feel like dancing. This bhava samadhi trance state was intended to be an intermediate stage on the way to meditation—an inducement to proceed on the spiritual path. In the same way that children are given a lollipop to entice them to go to school. Unfortunately, due to misunderstanding, many have taken the lollipop but forgotten to go to school! Worse still, certain individuals have exploited this misunderstanding for selfish purposes who claimed in the bhava state that they were gods and goddesses, so as to manipulate and control others. This is not the spiritual school Swamiji intended. Many have become stuck on lollipops and don't realize that one needs to meditate after this stage has been reached. Similarly, in the 1980's some people claimed they were possessed by Swamiji and after his Mahasamadhi in 1994, some even claimed, "I am Swamiji." But Swamiji never said He would come through any particular person. He said, "I am everywhere." He told all to go within, and you would find Swamiji there.

Swamiji told this story to illustrate the proper relationship between a Guru and a disciple, when that disciple also becomes a Yogi. A father has a son. That son becomes a father himself one day, but he still remains a son to his father. So when a disciple of mine does Tapas and becomes a Yogi, that person does not become my Guru. He'll still be my disciple. No one can take the Guru's place. Despite this there is now fighting among factions and different groups of Swamiji's devotees. There are a number of websites all claiming that Swamiji speaks through them, with certain people saying, "I am Shivabalayogi." In truth, Swamiji does not come through any particular person, or come from anywhere, or go to any place. Swamiji is everywhere, one with the Divine. He gave us the darshan of Ardanarishwara—the dual Divine, masculine and feminine form of Shiva and Parvati—but he never claimed he was God. Once a Yogi has achieved Self-Realization, he is worthy of being worshiped as God, because such a being has lost all imagination of the ego, and is one with the Self as taught in the Yoga Vasistha.

Hanuman was once asked what his relationship with Rama was. He replied that when he was in the bhava of duality, Rama was his master and he was Rama's servant. However, when in non-dual bhava,

Hanuman declared, "I do not exist. Only my Lord Rama exists." Swamiji worshiped Lord Shiva as his Guru. Once I called Swamiji, "Yogishwara", meaning "Lord of Yogis," but he told me not to use that word. "Don't call me that," He said, "call me Yogendra!" So the people making all these wild claims that Swamiji comes through them are like half-baked beans! Let me explain the term Mahasamadhi. A Guru in Mahasamadhi means He is in the supreme state of total mental stand-stillness, without any wavering. As long as the mind functions, it is wavering. The Divine has no resolutions of mind, so we cannot hold the Divine responsible for "bad" things that happen. If God had resolutions, then He would be partial. This earth was created by the Divine so all could be happy, but the human mind is such that unhappy people want to take away the happiness of others who are happy out of jealousy. Once a Yogi drops his physical body he has attained Mahasamadhi—oneness with the Divine.

A Yogi is what is known as a Jivanmukta, one who is liberated while still alive. A minimum amount of consciousness is required, so that the mind can interact with the world and operate the mission. This is known as the satvic ego, meaning a righteous ego, retained purely to serve the Divine. I have an attachment to Shivabalayogi. This is an ego manifestation, but if this were not present, this body would die, and we couldn't do our mission work. The Divine has ordained that we must teach spiritual knowledge and wisdom to the people, so the physical body needs to be maintained to continue the mission of Shivabalayogi. It's hard to believe that such great souls like Shivabalayogi actually existed—a Yogi who did twelve years of Tapas, and whom we observed for twenty years. He is everywhere, in your heart, within you. This is the truth. Once the Guru's grace descends, our mind must recede and become peaceful. We must gain consideration for others and overcome greed, anger, avarice, attachment to material things, false pride, and jealousy. If someone egotistically thinks, "I am Durga!" and another claims, "She is not Durga! I am Durga!" What is this, but the mind's pride and deceit?

Nobody saw Lord Shiva appear to Swamiji as a young boy, but thousands did witness the transformation of a young village boy into a great Yogi, filled with knowledge and wisdom. He could never really punish anyone, but people who did not understand Him left Him. You would always feel so serene at His Lotus Feet. Yes, He did Tapas. Learn to forgive one another and consider others. Don't become ruthless in the name of discipline. If you meditate, your prayers will be successful. If you are contented, you are like an emperor. One becomes poor through desires, like a billionaire always concerned about how to acquire more wealth. Reassure yourself that God will help you, that you are that Immortal Soul, and that you have that Eternal Peace. Practice so you will overcome the mind and attain perfection.

Meditation is a purifying process, where all the acquired negativities in the mind get evaporated. Don't be alarmed by this. The brain reflects into visions and thoughts. All this is getting purified; just don't analyze what happens. When meditating, we go beyond the duality of good and bad. Just keep watching and the mind will recede. The mind has got involved too much in the world. Its basis is really pure consciousness. Realized people become quiet. A Yogi conveys His real message through silence. Meditate first with patience and determination, and don't give excuses like you have to do other things—like go to a wedding ceremony, or attend a conference.

There is a story for this. Once Narada heard a devotee declare, "I want liberation!" Narada went to the devotee and told him that if he wanted liberation he should come with him at once, but the devotee explained that he was just married and wanted a son and now was not a good time. Narada returned many years later when his son arrived, but the devotee now explained that he didn't want to leave yet because he wanted to see his son grow up and so kept delaying, until Narada wondered whether the devotee really wanted liberation at all. You have to ask yourselves if you really want the Guru for peace and happiness. Be sincere to this meditation, practice it regularly. My Guru always stressed that it wasn't necessary to go to caves and forests. Twenty-three hours are yours for all your worldly needs. Just devote one hour every day to this meditation. Then it becomes a way of life.

Single-Pointed Attention Is Necessary On Every Spiritual Path

Dhyana (single-pointed attention) is important in every path. Spiritually, whether you are going on the path of bhakti and worship or any other method, our attention, concentration of the mind, is essential. Even if you want to serve the humanity physically, as in serving and helping the poor, the handicapped, terminally ill people, and so on, your service gets converted into sadhana only when you are able to offer all your services to the Supreme Being, God. Offering to God means, not simply through an utterance of words through your mouth. It should be sincere and your attention should be mentally on the Divine Guru, God. My Father, the Divine Guru has always said, "I will test for your sincerity and real devotion. I will test your ability to focus your attention on me." So Dhyana is important. Otherwise you will end up becoming more egotistic and arrogant, and everything will be simply a show business and it will take you nowhere.

In the bhakti path also, unless you are able to focus your mental attention on my Father, the Divine Guru, your worship or bhakti will be useless. Say you go to a place of worship or even at your home you offer prayers, flowers, incense, etc. At all times it is essential that your mind's attention be on the Divine. Otherwise, such a prayer and worship will be a waste of time and energy. Your attention on the Divine Guru is Dhyana. In bhakti you are trying to imagine the Divine Guru and in the process you always limit, because mind cannot show the Divine Guru absolutely. This is because what mind does is only through its own imagination. Imagination cannot be absolute. Just like you cannot measure the Space and you cannot even imagine the Space as it is, absolutely. So even in bhakti path also your devotion will be completely successful only when you are able to lose all imaginations and become single-conscious and single-pointed. After this is possible, when you are able to surrender totally without any imaginations, then the Divine Guru will drink your ego and take you.

Many people start trying to meditate and abandon saying, "It is very difficult and not possible." In bhakti also the rule is that you should be able to concentrate your attention. There shall not be any other thought in your consciousness. Then, when you find yourself having other thoughts do you stop worshiping? No, I don't think so. You will continue worshiping in the hope that one day God, the Divine Guru, will shower grace. In the same way, when you sit to try to meditate, if you find it difficult, do not abandon the practice. Be determined once again; though it is very difficult, it is not impossible. Your faith in the name of the Divine Guru can work wonders. So, faith and devotion go together. If you have faith, you will be devoted; if you have devotion, you will have faith. Without the other, one will never be there. If you try and meditate regularly, you will automatically develop devotion, knowledge, wisdom, sincerity, contentment, and the most elusive peace. You will become conscious of your Real Self that is Immortal.

For faith, concentration and to be conscious of the Divine Guru, let me tell you the story of Saint Kanaka Dasa who lived in South India, in what is now the state of Karnataka, about 500 years ago, during the reign of Vijayanagara Kings.

He was a cowherd boy, innocent and honest. One day when he was on the outskirts of his village with his buffaloes, he saw some scholars worshiping God nearby underneath a tree. Attracted, the boy went and from a distance, with all his humility, prostrating before them prayed to them to teach a way, so that he could also worship and know God. The learned scholars, out of false pride and arrogance, laughed at him and said, "Your friends and companions are buffaloes. What worship can you learn to know about God?" When the boy repeatedly prayed and requested, they cunningly told the boy, "Okay, let us see what you can do. Go and sit under the tree and repeat, 'Buffalo, Buffalo'." Laughing, they went away. The boy, with all his innocence and total faith, considering them to be his Gurus, went and sat under a tree. With all devotion and concentration he started repeating, "Buffalo, Buffalo." The legend has it that the God of death, Yama Dharma Raja, appeared before him sitting on a buffalo and guided him as a torchbearer. By initiating the boy into the name Kesava—one of the names of Lord Krishna—ultimately he became a Realized Soul by doing Tapas. He came to be known as Kanaka Dasa.

Under the guidance of Lord Yama, the Death God, the young boy adopted Saint Vyasa Theertha as the Guru, who was a well-known saint of that time. In the Guru's ashram, other students always felt jealous of Kanaka Dasa and always held him in derision. One day, the Guru thought of teaching a lesson to those other students who always made fun of Kanaka Dasa. By giving one banana to each of the students, including Kanaka Dasa, the Guru said, "All of you listen. Today go out and eat this banana where nobody would be watching you and come back before sunset. Whoever comes first, finishing the banana, would get first prize." All the students went and one by one arrived after finishing the banana. After all had arrived, Kanaka Dasa had not yet arrived. Students were waiting impatiently with gossiping and making fun of Kanaka saying, "Oh, the venerable Guru gave such a simple task of eating a banana with nobody watching. This idiot Kanaka could not fulfill the Guru's orders." One said, "Hey! The Guru wanted to test our wisdom and certainly this Kanaka has failed. The Guru will definitely expel him from the ashram."

Finally after sunset, Kanaka Dasa came and kept the banana at the feet of the Guru. He begged for pardon saying, "Venerable Master, ever since you ordered in the morning that we should go and eat this banana where nobody watched, this humble servant of Your Holiness failed in the task that you entrusted. Master, I tried to the best of my ability to eat without being watched, but wherever I went and tried at the places where nobody else watched, to my amazement, Oh, Gurudeva I saw everywhere Lord Krishna—the Supreme Being was watching me, with all His smiles. Hence I failed because I could cheat everybody else but not God as I saw Him watching from the depth of hearts." All other students were stunned at this and felt terribly ashamed. Then the Guru ridiculed them by saying, "Look at Kanaka Dasa. When you all were wasting your energies in gossip and jealous acts, this humble disciple of mine was busy paying his attention—Dhyana—on The All-Pervading Omnipresent Supreme Being."

New Years Message :
We Belong To Each Other

One more year has passed, one more New Year. Greetings, good wishes are conveyed in the hope that the coming new year would bring peace and happiness, prosperity and enjoyment. Humanity needs to work for it. The world does not seem to have peace and very often we hear of violence and sufferings. Why? Often we forget that we belong to each other. When we belong to each other, we will have to live for each other. We have to consider about each other. If somebody says something, perhaps unpleasant, we feel hurt. But we forget that others may also feel hurt when we say something unpleasant. When you press the trigger you enjoy, but if the trigger is against you and you are going to be hit, then you feel the pain. Yet time and again we fail to understand others' pain. This is why there is no peace. If we want peace we need to practice peace.

If we have to practice peace, we need a mind setup. Mind needs to be pure and capable of considering about others' pain and suffering. We must dream genuinely of peace to the whole Universe. If you practice sadhana (efforts to achieve pure mind) for mind control, such as meditation, it can help in achieving purity of mind—the ability to consider about the welfare of the entire Universe. Only a pure mind can think of pure things like peace, happiness to all and harmonious living on this earth. We need to build a better world for the future generation—a world free of violence and unnecessary sufferings; a world free of greed and hatred; a world free of fear and ignorance; a world free of narrow-mindedness and selfishness.

Let us talk less and get into the job. Look into the depth of your mind. Is it really pure and capable of dreaming for the welfare of the entire universe? Do undertake sadhana to purify the mind. See if you can help others. If you cannot help, at least do not bother them. Pray to God for the welfare, peace and happiness of the universe. Pray for all the worlds. We do not know how many worlds there are. May peace and happiness be there for all.

A Story About Creation And Devotion

When the creation first occurred, either through God's intention or perhaps it just happened, the legend has it that in the beginning an enormous amount of consciousness erupted ferociously, which came to be known as Maharudra. As Maharudra came into existence, He naturally wanted to know who He was and shouted thus, "Who am I?" A voice came from within the space, asking Him to sit into lotus posture and closing the eyes, concentrate in between eyebrows. Thus Maharudra went into deep Mahasamadhi. Creation could not occur. Then, the Divine Consciousness made Vishnu come into existence, so that Vishnu shall become the protector of creation. Through Vishnu, Brahma came into existence to undertake the responsibility of creation. Along with the eruption known as Maharudra, enormous power and energy also erupted. As Brahma went on creating, everything got engulfed by this energy known as Adi Para Shakti (first invisible energy of God). Then Brahma and Vishnu, along with Sanaka, Sananda, Sanatkumara, and Sanatsujata—the four first Yogis who came into existence from the consciousness of Brahma—all together prayed to the Divine to manifest, taking this energy which was swallowing all creation as Mother—because Mother concept is the kindest, who would forgive Her children unreservedly and unconditionally. Knowingly or unknowingly, every creature is likely to commit mistakes and require forgiveness with the kindness of a Mother. As Mother manifested, She released the creation from her womb. From time to time Mother has assumed numerous forms and names to protect the pious and noble, though She punished the

(47)

wicked. With enormous kindness she liberated them also from the bondage of the world.

So this is also how we should behave. If we are in a group, say for instance, a committee, whether you are secretary, vice-chairperson or chairperson, your focus should not be on the authority that goes with the position. The focus should be on your responsibilities in that position, not in the authority. We need to forgive each others' mistakes, just as God, as the Mother, forgives us—whether the mistakes are intended or unintended. She forgives before being asked to forgive, even without being asked to forgive. Mother is honored very much in India.

People often feel that Guru is showing more attention to one person instead of another. If a devotee wants to come closer, then they have to approach the Guru themselves. Guru cannot approach unless He is invited. If one is to attract the Guru, for instance in a group, then one needs to show participation, dedication, sadhana (efforts to achieve) and service. These four are essential for one to attract the Guru: participation, dedication, sadhana and service. Without these, the devotee cannot progress and Guru cannot come close. It is up to the devotee. Veda Vyasa also recommends that one shouldn't come too close to a Yogi either. If one comes too close, then that reverence, which is very necessary, may disappear. We may think that the Yogi is just like a normal person. "Oh, he just eats and gossips like us." The reverence is essential to be able to receive the grace of God and Guru. So Vyasa says that one shouldn't come too close to the Yogi, but also he says that one shouldn't stay too far away either. Too close means we can lose the reverence that is so necessary to be able to receive the grace that is flowing. Too far means that we distance ourselves from Him, and again He can't reach us.

Bhima was once complaining to Krishna, that He showed favoritism to Arjuna, and that He was partial to Arjuna above all others. Krishna said to Bhima that it was not so. He wanted to show Bhima, so He took him to where Arjuna was sleeping. As Arjuna was sleeping, as his breath went in and out, he was simply reciting

Krishna's name, even while he was asleep. So Krishna pointed this out to Bhima and explained that it was not that He was partial to Arjuna. It was simply that Arjuna's mind was always focused on Him. So Krishna explained that He had no choice in the matter, He was simply drawn automatically to Arjuna by his devotion.

Seven Techniques For Dealing With Difficult Situations

1) There is a saying, "When you have jumped into a river, you cannot be concerned with the cold." So don't be bothered if there are thorns in this world. Be glad there are some roses among the thorns.

2) Consider that people *know not what they are doing*. If someone behaves poorly with you they are showing their character. Your character is what it is and cannot be diminished by someone else's poor behavior.

3) To ignore a person, who is angry and behaving aggressively, to not lose your own temper, is sometimes the best slap you can give them.

4) If someone is wrongly criticizing you or abusing you verbally, let it go. Remember that you have nothing to be ashamed of. What you are is more important than what that person thinks of you.

5) Remember that the final battle in this world is to gain control over your own mind. When a person is able to remain composed and not lose the peace, they are ready to realize. If a disturbed person bothers you, visualize that the Divine Guru has sent that person to give you further commando training for this battle.

6) If a conflict arises, do not let your own mind be the first casualty. Console yourself that the Divine Guru is in your heart, that the Divine Guru loves you and will protect you.

7) Immediately engage the mind in purposeful work. If the mind cannot be controlled, engage it in something positive.

Do Not Wait For Miracles, Put In Efforts Now

We are always looking for miracles because we don't want to put in efforts! Suppose I want an ashram here in Perth, I may be tempted to think that God will give me one because He is everywhere and all powerful, so why should I bother putting in efforts? Not so. In truth I can teach anywhere, even under a tree. There will always be somewhere available. My efforts must be there to teach people to undertake sadhana. Every word can have a meaning if carefully observed. Efforts can bring miracles.

Krishna said that the wisest one is the person who wants to realize the Atman—the Self or God. To do this we need to make constant efforts and then a miracle will happen—that person will gain peace. Difficulties, obstacles, and stress may be daunting but the pain of all these things is really the imagination of the mind. Like a valiant soldier on the battlefield who doesn't feel the pain of his wounds and fights on with vigor, we can confront difficulties on the battlefield of life if we adopt the right attitude. A Yogi is one who has put in efforts and remained unconcerned about the results. I talk about meditation so that you may become inspired, so that the highest truth may ultimately be yours one day. It will happen.

I have no worries at all. I am free from all cares. Your mind is always wandering. How can the mind's wandering be stopped? It takes constant practice. You must put in effort. To achieve anything in this world, whether it's learning how to drive a car or just cook a meal, efforts are required. Effort, not spoon feeding, brings miracles. The mind worries about the future. You worry, "Can I do it? Will I

(52)

succeed?" Reassure yourself, it will become easier. I am here to show you the practical steps you need to take to progress spiritually. I make students sit and meditate in front of me. I am ready to help you; all that matters is your attention. Put in efforts to control the mind and never feel bored until you reach the goal. Every day is like a battlefield but in the long run you will hit the target. Even if it feels like there's a long way to go, be reassured you will get there in the end!

You meditate to control the unstable mind, which goes into craving. This is the reason for unhappiness. Controlling the mind does not mean destroying it; you are simply taking control of the vehicle. You'll acquire Self-Awareness of your existence as the Immortal Soul beyond the body. There is hope. You are permanent—everything else is impermanent. Everything material will disappear one day—the earth, the sun—but you, the Self, will always be there. Practice and you will get the blessings of the Divine Guru.

During meditation you may have astral experiences or visions of various kinds, but these are not really important. They are all illusion. Ultimately you must return to the Real Self. You must remember this. Your mind might get frustrated. Meditate to attain the highest; your existence as the Immortal Soul is the greatest wonder. Vasistha tells Rama, "It is amazing, I see that Self everywhere. For me, only the Self is visible." God is all-pervading, but why does He seem to be invisible? How can God escape your notice? It is simply because of ignorance. Say someone comes into the hall without knowing who Baba is, never having seen him before, he won't know for sure Baba is here. If he comes to know who Baba is, he'll realize its Baba talking. Similarly, we will one day realize, "Oh, this is God, consciousness fully aware of its own existence—*chidananda swarupam.*"

All Are Potentially Eligible To Do Tapas

Yesterday someone asked if a householder could do Tapas and attain Self-Realization. The answer is yes, it is possible. Let us say you want to sit for an engineering exam; no one will ask you first if you are a doctor or not! Are you prepared for the spiritual exam? In the same way, anybody can do Tapas and get realized. No one will ask if you are married or not, the question simply is: are you prepared to do the Tapas or not? That is what counts. In history, several ordinary people have undertaken Tapas and become Realized Souls, including well known saints. What is needed is the correct preparation and your attention. Eligibility is a must and all are potentially suitable. Buddha was a householder, a married man, and had a son and a beautiful wife. He had so much detachment that he left all this behind. Buddha had great determination. He observed that many priests and scholars had gone to great lengths to hold extremely painful postures, starving themselves for days on end so that their bellies shrunk inwards to their own spine. Still they attained no peace. Buddha thought to himself, "Let me take the middle path; let me eat rice and curds." So he sat under the Bodhi tree and with great determination performed Tapas.

There is a story at the end of the *Mahabharata*, after the Pandavas won the battle. Yudhishthira felt guilty after the battle because he had killed his own kith and kin and was overcome with grief. He organized an Aswamedha sacrifice, which involved leaving a horse free to roam far and wide in the countryside to show his supremacy as a ruler. Anybody who wanted to challenge his supremacy had to tie down the horse and then fight with the emperor. He invited people of all countries and religions to attend a fire sacrifice. Gifts and donations were to be distributed by the emperor. Strangely, a long tailed squirrel with a golden upper body suddenly appeared. It laughed and speaking like a human being, said it was happy that the fire sacrifice was being performed, but pointed out that the gifts and donations being distributed were much less than those received by a Brahman priest it had known long, long ago.

This was astonishing and everyone wondered how the creature could say such a thing? Yudhisthira had given everything away and all the appropriate mantras were recited. He had performed the ritual according to the prescribed rules laid down in the scriptures without any error at all. At that point the squirrel tells the whole story.

"Before the *Mahabharata* war there was a Brahman who lived in Kurukshetra with his wife and children. They always divided their meals into four equal servings. They offered the extra portions to others without asking for anything in return. They shared what they had equally, and even gave away to others beyond their means. They lived a life of the highest virtue, known as unchavriti. One day a calamity occurred. There was a severe drought and everyone was plunged into famine. Nevertheless they still remembered God's name and divided their one pound of maize flour into four equal shares to make chapattis. Just as they were getting ready to eat, a Brahman priest entered the small hut. The couple were such generous people that they were happy when a guest arrived unannounced. They washed the priest's feet and asked if he was hungry. They showed him what food they had available saying 'If you would take this and eat it we would be very grateful.' The priest took his share of flour and ate it, but appeared unsatisfied. The man's wife offered her portion and said, 'My Lord, please take this as well.' The Brahman refused, saying that he had no right to take her share as well. The wife insisted that it was her duty to look after the Brahmin. There was arguing and pleading and finally she gave the food to the unsatisfied Brahmin."

The squirrel continued his strange story saying that God had actually come in disguise to bless this couple. These people were so happy when they gave things away, such was their generosity. "Now," said the squirrel, "some of the flour had spilled onto the ground and I tried to sniff it but wherever the flour touched my body it turned to a golden color!" The squirrel explained that whenever a large ceremony is organized and gifts are given, he always wanted to see if it matched the quality of generosity he had witnessed in that couple. "So far, it hasn't happened," said the squirrel. "That's why I laughed when I heard how wonderful Yudhisthira fire sacrifice was supposed to be!"

Dharma had come to test Yudhisthira. The *Mahabharata* has such stories of virtue and sacrifice. We must try to consider the needs of other human beings ahead of our own. These days we kill to eat. We need to be taught such virtues so we can learn to live a life of virtue and chastity in this world. If humans have consideration for each other, we will be happy. We need to practice the austerities of real worship and meditation. Meditation is done to control the mind. Now the mind is totally distracted and it very quickly deviates from the path, from the goal. It wavers in its determination and dedication. We often lose patience. The mind causes us confusion, fear, chaos and unhappiness. Meditation is taught to control the mind. The mind is your own conscious energy; it doesn't need destroying, just taken control of. As the mind becomes purified, it loses its imaginations.

In ancient India the great saints regained Self-Awareness after having purified their minds and discovered how they existed as the Immortal Soul beyond the body, which continues to exist when the body dies. The consciousness of one's own existence, knowing the Self, can be achieved through meditation.

Don't Be A Slave Of The Mind

The first time creation took place, the form of Rudra appeared. As Rudra appeared in the space, He shouted, "Who am I?" An invisible voice came from the same space and asked Him to concentrate in between the eyebrows and meditate to know who He is. Then Rudra went into samadhi. Reproduction takes place, but no one happens to know whom we actually are. We generally think we come from our parents, but we are sucked into the worlds. We are mad after the world. The mind makes us a slave, which like money is a good servant but a very poor master. If you allow it to, it will run after what it wants like a monkey. How can you control it? It is a spark of your Real Self or God. It is a bundle of thoughts, you call mind. Which are actually the brain's effects and which are the mind's effects? It is very difficult to give a conclusive answer. You actually do what occurs to your mind. That's why discrimination is needed.

With meditation, prayers will be of the highest quality. If the mind is controlled, it does not matter what path you take, you will be guided from within. The mind is so often ahead of itself, trying to fool itself with its own illusions and imaginations. If the mind is controlled, you'll be able to solve problems and remain happy and peaceful. Ultimately you will also come to know the truth of God and the Real Self. When you achieve Realization, your mind settles in the Self and you are free from desires. You no longer feel you need to get any particular thing in order to attain happiness. You'll exist in a state of supreme happiness at all times. You need to experience this in order to believe it! If you practice regularly, He will listen to your prayers and you will reach Him soon. Yes, there is an all-pervading substance. Even after the death of this body, you will be supremely peaceful. This is what happens to a Yogi. Don't panic, progress step by step.

Shri Ramakrishna used to say that loving God means to accept God as He is. A child sitting with his father wouldn't ever think, "I'll love him for the property or wealth he may give me." Love God as God, and don't worry about what His boons are. To do so is low quality love. Don't think, "God has millions of dollars, so if He gives me sixty dollars, then I'll love Him." These conditions stop us loving God. There shouldn't be a business aspect to our relationship with the Divine! The sages of ancient times went on a quest for knowledge for its own sake, not for any ulterior motive. They dedicated their lives to the cause of Truth and gave humanity the Vedas and the Upanishads. Real devotion means we don't think about what God can do for us or what He can give.

"This World Is A Village Of Dead Bodies."
Saint Kabir

I offer my unconditional surrender at the lotus feet of the Divine Guru Shivabalayogi, who taught me and trained me in the path of the Yoga of Knowledge. The knowledge referred to here means: the Knowledge of the Ultimate Truth. With this kind of knowledge you don't actually need anything else. Knowers of the truth have attained it not by listening to someone else or attending lectures. This knowledge is the same as knowledge of the Self. To gain this knowledge you need to control the mind. How can one actually control the mind? That is the million dollar question. The mind is continually getting attached to sense objects. It keeps creating more and more imaginings uncontrollably, but all the objects that the mind gets attached to are transitory and therefore illusion. Instead of illusion you need happiness. The mind is looking for happiness. It's like the chicken and the egg; it's difficult to decide which came first, the illusion or the mind.

Skillfully you need to withdraw the mind. The brain is a physical organ and you need to keep it healthy. Don't disturb its function with unnatural things like alcohol and drugs. If these were the appropriate means to make progress, we would all be Yogis! You need to control the brain's reflections naturally. Alcohol and drugs will not enable the mind to lose its acquired habits. You need to apply your wisdom to determine what is real and what is unreal.

In the *Mahabharata*, Yudhishthira was asked by an angel, "What is the greatest mystery in the world?" He replied that the greatest mystery was that everyone knows that the body has to die one day, yet no one ever thinks about it. People think they will live forever! Just imagine how concerned you would be if you found out you had to lose an organ. It is part of your body and you value it so much, yet who thinks of losing the body? I don't mean that you should worry excessively about death and get depressed. Just apply your wisdom before this happens! Detachment is not the same as depression. Depression is a state of mind in which we are unable to accept the truth. The body must die, but the mind is unable to accept this truth. Detachment means being able to accept facts mentally and be ready to face up to them. Discriminating between the real and the unreal will help you to withdraw your mind from sense objects. Think about the transient nature of all objects.

The great Saint Kabir composed a famous poem on this theme.

This world is a village of dead bodies. The emperor must die, the commoner must also die. This earth will vanish, the sun and moon also. Even the creator of all the fourteen worlds and the Gods and Goddesses, and all their forms will disappear. Only the Self is eternal.

The mind has billions of layers, it has become puffed up. You need discrimination and dedication to bring it back to its source. It is possible. Practice the meditation regularly. The mind itself needs to learn that it is futile to run after illusory objects. You don't have to give up your way of life in this world. Skillfully go on. It's no problem if you are a householder, you can still earn a living. Start practicing meditation and you can withdraw the mind and still live peacefully and happily by applying your wisdom. Why is the practice of meditation needed? Can there be happiness without peace? If the mind is uncontrolled, it is not single-pointed. It keeps wavering. Right now, some of your attention is on Baba but ninety-nine percent is wandering. Try to keep your attention here. That is meditation. You need to pay 100 percent attention; otherwise the process of realization is slowed. Realization may take fifty-five or 55,000 lifetimes to achieve, depending on the potency of your attention. Control the mind by focusing your attention, then the mind becomes single-pointed. In this way, all illusions vanish and you are at peace at all times. Then you experience happiness. Worldly things can give only temporary happiness. For example, while you're eating an ice cream you're happy as long as it lasts, but then it's gone. Temporarily the major focus of your attention is on the ice cream, but you are also imagining the ice cream! It doesn't give any happiness. Actually, you're only happy because your mind is there. Once it's gone, the happiness is over.

When the mind is withdrawn, what happens to it? How does it gain knowledge of the Self? People worry what will happen to them if they stop thinking. They get frightened and think they should start meditation later when they're in there seventies. Well, if they wait that long they'll have to face problems like arthritis, problems in the cervical spine and so on. Don't wait until then when it may be difficult to sit and meditate. Don't worry, when the mind recedes it does not vanish, it is immortal and infinite. The mind is a permanent entity; it gets absorbed in the Real Self like a droplet merges with the ocean.

Just imagine if the mind can get so much happiness focusing on an ice cream, what peace and bliss it can experience if it is absorbed in the Self. This is described as *Brahmanandam Paramasukhadam*— the Supreme Peace beyond all imaginations, which has no equal. This happens as the mind is absorbed in the Self and all imaginations stop, like a salt doll is dissolved when immersed in the ocean. This can happen if you practice meditation. You can live peacefully and happily in this world. The human mind in its ignorance becomes destructive when it looks outside for happiness and acts like an emperor; it starts conflicts, which would even spread beyond the earth to other planets given the chance! Let the mind find true peace in the Self and become constructive, for you are actually the abode of that Supreme Peace.

If You Want To Know Who You Are, It Must Be A Priority

May you be inspired to be in the company of good people and perform sadhana to control your mind. My Guru felt the need to take meditation practice to every corner of the world, to anyone who wants to learn. It wasn't always so easy to get this knowledge. In ancient times one attended a gurukulum, where the teachers taught spiritual practices and the students performed this sadhana. These ashrams were away from the towns and cities in forests where the sadhaks led a simple life. There were hardships in those days, communication and traveling was very arduous. My Guru's attitude was to let anyone who wants this teaching have it. He received permission from Lord Shiva to initiate anyone into the meditation, anyone of any age. He was directed to teach in a simple way.

How can the mind go to meditation while in the midst of worldly duties? If a person is ready to become a monk and sage then one can devote the maximum time, if one has no other duties. Living in the world means you need to earn a livelihood so you can buy food, have a place to live and a respectable life can be led. In India we were taught to get up early to perform rituals, repeat God's name and attend to various duties. These days stress levels have increased, job demands are greater. Now the basic aim of most people is to just earn as much money as possible. The greed of humanity has increased; there is no limit to how much money people want these days. The pressure to increase earnings has become such a stress that the physical body is weakened. It's difficult for people to sit peacefully, they are so busy. People brush aside the need to do meditation, saying they must work ten hours, that they have to go to bed very late, etc.

If you want peace, if you want to reduce stress, if you want to know who you are, you need to take out the time as a priority. If you had the opportunity to earn a million dollars, you'd certainly take out the time, even if it meant losing sleep for several days. You must ask yourself what your true requirement is for your peace and happiness. Every day when your body and mind is healthy and you only try to earn money, you lose peace and happiness. There appears to be no way out. You just have to tune the mind to meditation, it is essential.

If you want to come and see Babaji, you need to take time out. Very often people don't value things unless they pay for them, but we help people to do spiritual practice without charging them. It's simple really—eat to live, don't live only to eat. We must come off the wrong path we have taken. Remember the Guru and take out at least forty-five minutes for meditation every day. There is plenty of time remaining for you to do your other tasks. People mistakenly think they can sit back and expect God to give them everything; they don't need to do anything at all. This is wrong. God never gives spoon feeding like that! You are in this world, so you face the dualities and stresses of the world and become confused, so you need take out the time for meditation.

I have been asked what the definition of a selfless action is. A selfless action is whatever we do for the true Self only. You try to do things for as large a cause as possible. Let us surrender to God, let us give selflessly, come one and all, take this knowledge and wisdom. Our giving the knowledge will not depend on the donations you may give. We give it freely.

Parents often become stressed about their children. These children are souls who you owe something to, so you have the chance to give them something back. God will look after the rest. Gradually try to see God everywhere. You will simply do everything as a duty and not worry about anything. "What if I don't get what I want?" This is what most people think. When things are performed as a duty, you can be selfless. The mind will not get involved in such actions.

I never tried to analyze why my Guru told me to do certain things—I just went ahead and did them. He wanted me to work, dust rooms, clean toilets, and look after mentally retarded children or children of rich devotees. People used to criticize what I was doing and the way of life I had chosen. They said I was wasting time like someone sitting under a tree. They told me to get married. I did not leave home to escape from work. I received no VIP treatment living at the ashram; I went there only interested in losing my own ego to get the Ultimate Truth.

Why should a Guru only teach in one particular way? He makes the disciple do all sorts of odd things. Let the mind not bother about it, let it recede. Surrender, so it doesn't go into agitations. Let it remain quiet and meditate. Perform all the physical work necessary, then as devotion and faith increase, you will have peace. My mind never observed all the physical work the body was doing. The mind was remembering the Guru even while working. Unknown to the world we meditated for twenty years. The world only observed the last five years! People noticed me only then. They thought, "He is sitting in a room doing Tapas!" While cleaning toilets and doing all kinds of menial jobs, I kept on meditating. People assumed I was a low quality devotee because of the kind of work I used to do. If you can live like this in the world you will be benefited. Just do the work and think that the Guru made me do these things.

Take the time to meditate forty-five minutes every day. The great Saints, Shivabalayogi and Ramana Maharshi used to say there is no need to run to forests and caves. If you run there before you are ready, you'll just carry all the weight of your mind with you! A brother disciple of mine gave up after three years of Tapas. He ran away distressed, even though the Guru was physically available. Get trained first. Do the practice. When the time is ripe, the chance will come. My Guru was observing me the whole time I was working. He told me my mind had the ability to become quiet following the service I had done and counted this work as seven years credit towards Tapas. He said the five years of Tapas would be easy for me. The mind was ready and prepared.

It Is True We Are Dreaming;
It Is Not True The Dream Is Real

I have been trying to make you know the truth about the mind, the world and the need for mind control—the truth about the real versus the unreal. These teachings are the same as those in the Vedas, the need to discriminate the real from the unreal. This is a most difficult task. For this purpose we have a human body—which is a rare gem—and a wonderful brain.

What do we require to attain permanent happiness? We think it is money, a home, the planet earth or this body. But if we analyze things properly we see that none of these things, including our own physical body can give permanent happiness. Everything is transitory. When a thing is not permanent, how can it give permanent peace? Only something that is permanent and immortal can give happiness and peace.

The great poet Saint Kabir put it quite bluntly when he called this planet earth a village of dead bodies. I am not so blunt; I tend to speak softly and try to convert people with positives. All that is needed is that you remain alert. I used to sing this song by Kabir and I was ridiculed for it. The song, in part, goes: "Nobody seems to be alive, except the Supreme Consciousness, the life current which flows in all, thanks to which everything appears to be alive." Be alert, you come from the abode of the Divine. You have to be ready to leave also. Many saints have said this. My Guru said to do one hour of meditation and you have twenty-three hours left for normal life—no problem. Take up this practice and sit in meditation for one hour. You'll find it so peaceful, wherever you are and whatever you do— that is your duty. Give it as a service to the Divine.

We try to discriminate the real from the unreal. It's very difficult when the unreal appears real. Just like when you are dreaming, you can't discriminate what is real and what is not. This life is a long dream. When you wake up after a bad dream you thank God that the terrible dream is over and feel relieved. We reassure ourselves that it was just a dream and that no one is really out to get me, and so on. We discriminate in this way and we realize that though the dream really happened, the things in the dream were imaginary. This gives happiness and satisfaction. But we are unhappy when the things of the dream appear real. So it is with normal life. The correct attitude should be, "Let me play this role in waking life, no problem." Thinking like this, even if ten wicked people try to torment you, you won't be disturbed.

The story of the great devotee Prahlada illustrates this. His father was a demon and used to taunt Prahlada saying, "Where is your God? He doesn't exist." Prahlada replied that his father considered his body as God, which was a complete illusion. God is everywhere. If Baba says, "I am realized," then says, "God is here but not there," Baba can't be realized. But Baba says God is everywhere. That's the Divine play. Prahlada was fearless. His father was amazed and became angry, shouting that Prahlada was his son. He proceeded to threaten him saying, "I say I am God. Your God doesn't exist. I will put you to death!" Prahlada's father tried to kill his son in several ways. He tried to throw the boy from a mountain top, tried poisoning him, even threw him in boiling oil, but Prahlada remains fearless. In the legend the Divine protects the boy every time and finally appears from a pillar.

The demons also did Tapas but their goal was different. They used to spend their money and energies on alcohol and other vices. A saint will use any acquired money for good causes. A Yogi prays to the Divine to give happiness to the people, that they may love each other. The demons pray only for power, so they can be called

Gods. If you have 100 percent concentration, God will appear in response to prayers. If you ask for a boon, you are likely to ask for the equivalent of chocolate, yet God is ready to give a whole supermarket to you! The demons prayed for boons like immortality, and attached all sorts of clever conditions to cover all possibilities. For example, they would pray, "Let me not die in the sky, nor in the earth, neither by day nor by night," and so on. Finally God came in the form of a half-lion and half-human, known as Narasimha. God came in that form at such a time to destroy the demon with his own claws.

The story of Nachiketa tells of the young boy who quizzed the God of death, Yama, about the truth. Nachiketa's father was a great scholar and used to say that there was no birth and no death. One day the boy saw his father preparing for a fire sacrifice and afterwards all the learned priests would be sent away with the proper gifts. The boy asked his father why he was making a list and his father cursed him, calling him an idiot, saying he would gift him to the God of death. Now Nachiketa was honest and obedient and he later reminded his mother and father that he had been promised to the God of death. At this his father became terrified and wept that Nachiketa was his only child, and cried out, "How will I go on living when Nachiketa dies?" Nachiketa felt disgusted at his father's hypocrisy and at the appointed time, jumped into the fire to reach the abode of the Yama. His father had preached the truths of non-duality but had not been able to practice them. He used to say, "You are eternal, you are not going to die." But when death came to his boy he forgot all that wisdom.

Yama was pleased with the boy's honesty and wisdom and offered three boons. Nachiketa, concerned about his father's regret, asked that no blame be put on his father for having wished him to the God of death. Secondly, he asked for a mystery to be solved. "Everyday my father used to discourse about life after death—how we are really the Atman, the Immortal Soul—yet how to know this for sure? I saw my father suffer, despite saying all this. What is the truth after all?" Yama tells the boy not to worry about such questions and offers him the chance to become emperor of the world for ten thousand years, saying he would be able to have many wives, unlimited power, obedient subjects and so on. Nachiketa just wanted to know one thing. He asks, "After the ten thousand years, will I have to come back here to you? Can I ever avoid coming back to you, even after fifty thousand years? Tell me the truth. I may not remember then, so tell me now." Finally, seeing the determination of the young boy, Lord Yama tells him the truth that he will have to come back to face him no matter how long a mortal life he has been given. This is the story of the great scripture, the Katho Upanishad.

The third boon Nachiketa asks for is Yama's blessing that Yama be his Guru. Yama said, "I will tell you the truth only once, so you must pay attention to me." Nachiketa was receptive to his Guru's teachings and eventually attained samadhi according to the story. It illustrates overcoming illusion and the discrimination of the real from the unreal. The mind must merge back into the Self once it has lost all its imaginations, just like the droplet of water merges back into the ocean. The mind is restless and distracted. The mind's imagination is an amazing expression of your own conscious energy. Just control your imagination. Don't start thinking that your imagination is real.

God appeared to my Guru when he was fourteen years old. People may ask where the evidence is that He saw God, but this is a manifestation of the heart. My Guru achieved such a level of concentration; he attained the state of total thoughtlessness, of mental stillness. He never read any scriptures, couldn't give lectures, and spoke no English, only his mother tongue and a smattering of other Indian languages, so that he always had an interpreter. He spoke about faith, devotion, and how devotion can work miracles. If you have faith in the Guru, even the Guru cannot disturb you. In 1978, I asked Swamiji for his Vibhuti blessing to go into Tapas. He told me to have faith. Much later he initiated me into Tapas. I had faith. I never thought I could sit for so many hours. Have faith and determination and you too will be able to do this meditation.

Two Friends—the Brain And The Mind

It is the knowledge of the Self and true wisdom that we seek. The Self is the Abode of Peace. Our real nature is peace. Look at the friends brain and mind. Though it is very difficult to tell which came into existence first, what seems to be a good relationship gives way. The mind suffers at the hands of its friend. The brain is an amazing organ in the body that has enabled the soul to be conscious and aware of the universe—to be able to live in this world, work, eat, and live. Enjoyment is the thing that you are looking for. The brain is in touch with the nervous system and the universe. Through its reflections, the mind, which is a spark of the Supreme Consciousness called the Self, comes into existence. This mind assumes everything that is reflected by the brain is real, recognizes and absorbs as an imprint, and starts wandering in the universe aimlessly—getting pampered, losing control, losing consciousness of Self.

Everything the brain reflects seems so real. We have acquired so many reflections. Since a small child, through youth and old age, the mind clings onto these reflections, and so peace seems to be an illusion. The brain has taken the mind away from itself. Craving of the mind is the reason for all unhappiness in the world. To overcome this we need to meditate. This mind is your child. If mind is unhappy, you are unhappy. If the mind is peaceful, then you are peaceful. Actually, the mind is missing and is looking for that Supreme Peace which it had always enjoyed while one with the Real Self. Attention to the world always results in tension. Mind requires an anchor—somewhere, somebody to show the way for the mind to go back to the Self. You cannot depend on the world for peace and happiness. Nothing is permanent. Everything is transitory—morning changes to night, the body changes from being a child to an adult and then old age. This is not something to be feared. It is natural.

To overcome fears and tension the basic aim is to quieten the mind, which has gone into millions of imaginations. Just like a spider gets stuck in the web, the mind has hypnotized itself. You are not going to destroy the mind by practicing meditation. You need to practice stopping the mind, the same as you stop a car. When you do not want to drive it, you park it. When you want to drive the car again, you can. When you can control the mind, the brain will be your servant. Meditation practice to control the mind aids the ability to achieve peace and happiness. The brain is a biological, amazing organ in the physical body. It can be a good servant but a very bad master. You need to use the brain and not allow your spark of consciousness called the mind to get fooled by the reflections of the brain.

The Scorpion And The Saint

There is a story of a Saint who was taking his bath in a pond. A scorpion had fallen into that water, so the Saint put out his hand to save it. Due to its nature, the scorpion stung that Saint and fell back into the water. Again the Saint picked the scorpion out of the water and again was stung. Finally the scorpion fell into deeper water and was drowned.

The illusions in the world seem so real. People are tempted by name and fame. They want prestige and to be honored. At a certain point they cannot resist the temptation, due to their weakness.

Learn From Others And
Do Not Cheat Yourself

Remember Swamiji is within you. Your mind can take you to Him. These days' people waste their time and energies in nasty, useless criticism, finding fault with others. Jealousy is a common enemy. The six shapes of the mind: extreme greed, extreme anger, extreme stinginess, extreme attachment, extreme false pride (ego) and jealousy, trouble human minds as six main enemies. People should try to overcome these enemies; otherwise their own minds are the first casualty. When you want to learn something, be sincere to yourself and to the person from whom you want to learn. Swamiji taught that if somebody has knowledge that you require, do not hesitate to learn. Learn for the sake of acquiring knowledge. If you try to cheat, you will ultimately be cheating yourself. Saint Kabir said, "Rob the name of Lord Rama; rob as much as you can before death will take away your body."

One fine midnight, walking on the balcony of the Dehradun Ashram, Swamiji told me a funny story of a student who did not have reverence to the person from whom he wanted to learn but instead wanted to cheat the Master and beat him. Once upon a time, there lived a famous expert wrestler in a particular country. Nobody could beat him from near and far off places. But the wrestling Master was very humble and was ready to teach all, sincerely without any discrimination. There was a cunning man who lived near the town where the Master lived. This man one day came to the Master with an evil design. This man had thought, "If I can learn everything from this Master, then I can beat and humiliate the Master." As were the rules, if the Master refused a challenge he would have to accept defeat.

Sincerely, the wrestling Master taught the cunning man all the wrestling tricks with so many grips. Immediately after learning, the cunning man started showing his true colors. Straightaway, he went to the king and boasted that now he could beat the Master, as he had learned everything. The king thought, "This man seems to be cunning and has no reverence to the person who taught him." The king warned, "Oh, Man! This is not proper manners, that you boast of yourself and talk in a derogatory manner of the person who taught you." The cunning man replied, "So what if he had taught me, still he has to win over me in the wrestling competition." The king thought, "Now fate will decide." So the king agreed to the match and asked his minister to fix a date and inform the public.

On the fixed day, apart from the king, there was a very large crowd assembled to witness the fight. The cunning man went around boasting that within minutes he would beat the Master. The fight began, and for some time, as the cunning man was young, he appeared to be strong and winning. But suddenly the Master applied a strong grip trick and to the amazement of the crowd; the young, cunning man lay on the ground defeated and bruised. The cunning man complained, "Oh, Master! You have cheated me! You never taught me this particular grip trick." Smilingly the Master said, "Fool, I knew you would try to be cunning, to acquire your own fame by humiliating me. Know that I have so many of these grip tricks to show at the right time and place for cunning people like you."

Fate, Free Will, God's Wishes :
Surrender The Agitations Of Mind

Things are happening in this world, not according to God's wishes, but due to God. God has no mind and no thought, just like light is due to the sun but not due to the sun's wishes. That is why God has no partiality, just like the sun has no partiality, whether to give light to some and not to give to others. Whichever object comes in front of the sun, the light is given. Whoever can pray and surrender mentally can get God's blessings. This is what I mean when I say not to analyze mentally so that the mind may surrender to God. It has no third way. Either it is wandering in the world with imaginations, analyzing and making judgments or it will be going towards God.

When you take it as free will, also it is due to God. When you take it as destiny, it is also due to God. This dualism will go on in this world. When you consider it free will, where is that free will coming from? It is from the Divine only. Suppose you want to do according to your free will, still you are doing according to the inspiration that is coming. How can you be free? That is why when you have to think and work, you have to pray to God to inspire you. You should not abandon karma; only the results are to be taken as destiny or God's grace. All the dualism of good and bad are God's play. If God is in Rama, God is in Ravana also. But you can overcome these effects of dualism only when you achieve samadhi.

While you shall work for good in this world, you need to take care that your mind does not get involved too much into analyzing bad things and wrong things. The Guru guides you gradually to overcome these dualism effects, so that you can get liberated. That is when you rise above both good and bad. This is what I mean when I urge devotees not to go on analyzing too much. Best is, if you can simply surrender and go according to Guru's guidance, because the Guru knows Karma Rahasya, the secret of karma and its fruits. That is why Shri Krishna told Arjuna not to bother about anything. "They are already dead. You just take your bow and shoot arrows." Such surrender to the Guru can keep a disciple's mind free from any imaginations. The devotee thinks, "Let me mentally not analyze why the Guru is saying so, and just do what the Guru says. He knows better." Thus the devotee's mind stops getting agitated.

When you plan anything, you are actually playing into the hand of fate. Listen to your inner voice or to the ordainment of the Guru in reacting to situations. The Guru wants to help you to lose imaginations and definitions, so that your mind can surrender to God-Consciousness gradually and get liberated. Because when death occurs to the body, the next birth depends on the acquired habits of the mind. If it keeps getting into agitations unnecessarily, that results in the next type of birth. I do mean it when I say it is a very difficult, rare life cycle to get a human birth, the brain of which has wisdom to listen to the Guru and lose ego. Animal instincts have no such ability, unless in rare cases, having come in contact with great saints, they have attained liberation. Ultimately you are made to think, you are made to do it. Whatever you do, you play into fate. Swamiji said, "If it has to come, it will come. Do not grudge." The basic idea here is, do not allow your mind to get agitated. This is what Baba teaches tirelessly again and again.

Yes, this hand of fate means both positive and negative, leading to rebirths. Where were you before being born in this life? Do you have any remembrance, any control over that? That is why one needs to pray to Guru and God, with total surrender and reverence of devotion, for guidance and blessings to get liberated. Gradually, as you surrender with love and devotion, your elevation towards God starts. See, only due to the samskaras (acquired habits of mind) of some immediate previous births, you are always attracted to Saints and their teachings. No matter to which place (tradition) you belong, or if the Saint may belong to some other place. That is why a Yogi is beyond boundaries of places and time. A Yogi belongs to all. Notice now, gradually this is leading you to acquire higher knowledge of the Truth. Sometimes, when you meet a Yogi, you develop an attachment of love and devotion unknown to you. You adopt such a Saint, such a Yogi as your Mother, Father, and Guru. Are all these in your hands? It happens.

Doing sadhana can be pre-ordained, but one should notice this properly. When the time is ripe, the Guru comes as the messenger of God. Guru gives Upadesham (ordainment that needs to be noticed as God's pre-ordainment). If the mind prays to God, it is able to notice. Otherwise, mind wanders into worldliness and fails to notice. Karma of prayers, determination to obtain Guru's and God's grace is needed. Once my Guru said, pointing at me, "Look, even if I cut this boy into pieces and throw them into the river, he will come back joined. That is the boy's faith and determination." Thus very often God gives a chance to every soul to overcome the effects of illusion. As parents, God guides. As friends, God helps. As enemies, God keeps us alert. As the Guru, God guides and takes you in His boat to cross the ocean of samsara. One has to utilize the opportunity, jump into it. That is why Baba urges devotees to stop analyzing mentally and surrender mentally, so that all agitations of the mind can stop.

This is what Lord Krishna taught Arjuna, essentially, in the discourse of Bhagavad-Gita. Very often, even such a mighty soul like Arjuna could not understand easily. Even when he understood a little bit, he said, "Lord, my mind is so restless, so wandering. How can this stop?" But there was one positive, clinching point in Arjuna, which was his love and devotion to Lord Krishna. Though very often he argued with Krishna—irritated the Divine Krishna. With his foolish definitions and analyzation, still he could not say no to the commandment of Krishna. Thus, the Lord ordained it to Arjuna, "Take the bows and arrows. They are already dead. Do not bother anything in the mind, just shoot and leave everything to me," Arjuna got up to shoot his arrows as guided by Krishna. Arjuna's mind had stopped agitating. It had surrendered to Krishna. Arjuna could see only Lord Krishna everywhere in the battlefield. When he was totally into Krishna-Consciousness, he saw Krishna in Pandavas and in Kauravas. He saw Krishna leela (divine play) everywhere. His mind had got liberated from the agony of dualism.

If There Is No Job For The Mind To Do, It Will Recede

On the path of spirituality, one must be clear about the exercises and the target, to enable one to find the Truth. Otherwise, you might try to catch the wrong things. Over the whole world as I travel around, I see that spirituality flourishes. There is so much spiritual activity around the world, but still we don't see the results of spiritual efforts. Still we don't see changes in the human beings. We don't see the human beings being more loving, caring, considerate, and peaceful. We humans don't have a greater understanding of the spiritual truths. It is good to go into sadhana, but we must also know what and why and how to do it properly.

Swamiji spoke repeatedly about meditation for Self-Realization. When He had completed His twelve years of Tapas and came out, so many hundreds of thousands of people gathered to see the great Yogi come out into the world. He was requested to give a message to those gathered together. His message was, "Humanity has forgotten who they really are. They must remember who they really are." Ramana Maharshi spoke also, that only one single truth exists— a state in which there is no seen and seer. Adi Shankaracharya spoke the same thing as Advaita.

We think of God as separate to ourselves, that when God appears, then the sakshatkaram (direct realization of God) happens. But really it is when the mind loses all imaginations and merges with the Self. This is inexpressible; nobody has been able to define it. When the mantra for Shivabalayogi came, it was mesmerizing for me. Right through my life it has given me everything. So I saw God in the form of Shivabalayogi at the end of my sadhana, just before the 'I' merged into the Divine, just like a droplet merges with the ocean. Because the mind exists, it has given the imagination of 'I' and the 'world'. We want to enjoy the world by having it to ourselves. That is the problem. A Yogi realizes God is everywhere.

As an example, Guru Nanak as a child was helping His father in the shop, and was counting some items. As He counted up in Hindi, He reached the number thirteen, which is pronounced *Thera* in Hindi, a word that also means 'Yours'. When He got to that number, He kept repeating, "thera, thera," and His mind became so concentrated on the thought that all was God's, He became Realized. So this is how the mind gets involved, thinking everything in the world is ours, but even the body is not ours. One day He will take it back. Everything is God's. But even these things are hard to overcome. Like an alcoholic who takes a vow that he will not drink alcohol again, but the mind keeps going back to that habit. This is how the mind works. It keeps going back, jumping to one shape. So it is necessary to do sadhana.

Swamiji used to say, "Who are we to set right the world?" You have to first rectify yourself, your own mind. When the mind becomes right, then everything will appear all right. Look within yourself. Sometimes people talk of the third eye. This is actually your own mind. The mind has to be present and active, to activate all the senses. So for instance, if you don't pay attention to music that is playing, then you won't hear it. The mind's attention, when it becomes focused, comes to that point between the two eyes, and its perception is like a third eye. One needs to do sadhana and look within. Meditation is the blanket remedy for all our ills. Dhyana itself leads to Jnana (knowledge) and Bhakti (devotion). Finally when the Truth is revealed, then the Yogi will say, "Oh! So that is God," as Adi Shankaracharya expressed, *Aham Brahmasmi*.

Prahlada was ridiculed by his father, a demonic king, "Where is your God?" In Advaita philosophy, one will say that the body is

God, but the problem occurs when we think He is limited to only that body. The total surrender can occur only through Tapas. Through any sadhana the mind should recede. If the mind gets excited, it jumps back into the world, and any sadhana that does that, is a waste of time. In meditation, if the mind recognizes thoughts and visions, these are not the real experiences. The mind has billions of habits, samskaras, and when we meditate, the mind replays them and they can show as visions. When the vision occurs, the mind tends to recognize, analyze and then judges. So when you see a vision, the mind can get involved. In the same manner, the Yogi really doesn't see people as bad or good. The mind has to understand that it should not get involved; it should be just a witness, *Sakshi Bhutam*. So, when you are meditating, one should concentrate, focus and not get involved. One instruction given is, "Do not imagine anything." Don't imagine what it is. If there is no job for it, the mind will recede. Until that stage, when the mind recognizes something, it gets involved.

Mind or illusion, which came first? We can't know. There is no conclusive answer to this. In meditation, try to overcome the illusions in the mind. We are unable to control the illusion, so we control the mind. When we withdraw the mind, the illusion drops off. The mind has to remain quiet, and when that happens, only pure consciousness remains. The ancient sages have said that the Soul is immortal. There is one immortal Self, which is God. These are the same.

As long as there is ego, there are thoughts like, "I am this and I am that." When they stop, only the Real Self remains. Ramana Maharshi, when He was a young boy, went through a death experience, felt His body was gone, and tried to see what remained. Similarly with the senses, the mind, what remained? Only the Self, which is 'I' remains. And so when His family were all grieving and crying loudly at an uncle's funeral, He asked what they were crying for. He suggested that if His uncle was the body, then that was still there. If it is something else, then we really can't know what has happened to it. These sorts of things inspired me when I was young. If you really are interested, then God will send a Guru. Everyone these days wants to be the guru first. Swamiji used to say that we should try to be the perfect disciple first. If you are genuine, God will help; he will send the Guru to your doorstep. All that is needed is that you need to be sincere.

How To Function In The World While Remaining Aware Of The Divine

In Yoga Vasistha, the story of Sage Vyasa's son, Suka, is used to illustrate how one can function in the world, while maintaining an awareness of God. Once Suka came to his father, Vyasa, and asked him about this. Vyasa could see that, as Suka was his son, if he simply told him the answer, then it would not mean very much to him. So he told Suka that he should go to King Janaka to learn about this. He told Suka that Janaka, though a king governing a kingdom was a Realized Soul, and that Suka should approach him respectfully and ask to be shown this knowledge. So Suka came to Janaka's kingdom.

Now it was the practice in those days that teachers would test their students thoroughly before accepting them into training. So the king told his servants to keep the young man waiting at the gates until the king himself said it was time for him to be given an audience with the king. So Suka was kept at the gates it is said for three days—no food, no seat or bed, nothing. But the servants reported to the king that although they had not offered Suka all the normal courtesies which one would usually extend to such an honorable person visiting, that still Suka was behaving very well, and was not shouting or abusing anyone. So Janaka felt that he was a fit person to be taken as a student. So after the three days, the king told the servants to bring Suka into the court for an audience. The king asked Suka what he wanted. Suka said that he wanted to know if one could be Self-Realized and yet also still carry on their normal, proper functions in this world.

Janaka replied that he would be happy to teach this to Suka, but that this was a very important thing to understand, and that he was caught up at the present with some matters to do with governing the kingdom, and didn't have the proper time available right now to teach this to him thoroughly. So Janaka suggested that Suka come back in the evening, when Janaka would have the proper time available to discuss this topic more thoroughly. The king suggested that, to fill in the time until that evening interview, Suka go for a tour around the city to see what it all looked like. Janaka further suggested however, that while Suka toured around the city, he should keep a small lamp on his head, and that he should make sure not to lose the lamp, or spill it. So Suka went off for his tour while he was waiting to see King Janaka again in the evening. When he returned to see the king, Janaka asked him what he had seen of the city during his tour. Suka replied that as his attention was on the lamp, which he was balancing on his head, he had not taken very much notice of the things that were going on in the city around him. Janaka said that this was how he, himself, experienced the things of the world. As a Realized Soul his attention was always towards God, and yet he did move around and appeared to be engaged in the world.

Mother

Remember, when you commit a wrong act, even though nobody else may be able to see it, the mind stores the impression of that, deep in a corner of the heart. So Vasistha recommends meditation to clear this away. Today is Mother's Day. The concept of Mother is perhaps God's greatest concept. When the creation came out of the Divine, a tremendous eruption of consciousness, Rudra, occurred. With that consciousness, an enormous energy came out, engulfing the whole of creation. The huge fireball of energy threatened to consume the whole of creation. So Brahma and Vishnu together prayed to the Divine to convert this enormous energy into the concept of Mother. Mother will forgive unreservedly. This Mother is referred to as Adi Parashakti; 'Adi' meaning first, 'Para' meaning invisible, and 'Shakti' meaning energy. So, it is with gratitude to the Divine that we think of this, and honor the Mother. Mother is the kindest, but still when she sees the children on the wrong path, she will pull them up. In the same way, a Yogi is like a Mother and Father. He is affectionate like the Mother, but if we go on the wrong path and get caught up into the dualities of the world, then the Yogi will pull up His children as a Mother. The Guru is always an ocean of grace. If Guru shows he is annoyed, it is only to help. If he gets angry, it doesn't mean he rejects or destroys the child. A Mother will never reject the child. So we are grateful to God for the creation of the Mother. Just as every child is totally secure with the Mother, so also every soul is totally secure with the Guru.

The Real Guru Would Like You To Stand On Your Own Feet

We pay rich tributes to all the real Gurus of this world who have come from time to time in different parts of the world. The real way of paying tributes would be to do sadhana seriously, with a 'never give up' attitude and determined mind set to follow the path initiated by the Guru. When you get attracted to the Guru, gradually your mind must go introverted towards the Self. That is the grace of the Divine Guru. That means you are on the path perfectly. The great Maha Gurus, like Lord Krishna, Jesus, Buddha, Guru Nanak, and our beloved Guru Maharaj, Swamiji, all exist as one with the All-Pervading Omnipotent, the Divine, and Supreme Consciousness. When you pray to these Maha Gurus, the Divine will shower grace upon you.

It is the mercy of my true Guru that has made me to know the unknown. I have learned from the Guru to walk without feet, to see without opening the eyes, to hear the Truth without using the physical ears, to experience the Truth without the ego of identification. If the Guru is realized and you are receptive with sincerity, you will feel the Guru as a strong magnet with charisma. You will feel the gravitational pull towards the Guru, when you are sincere to the need of spiritual truth, the Self. The real Guru gives you liberation not make a slave of you. If the Guru tries to make a slave of devotees by feeding doctrines of philosophy, that is certainly not a Satguru, Maha Guru or Guru at all. The one who wants you to experience the

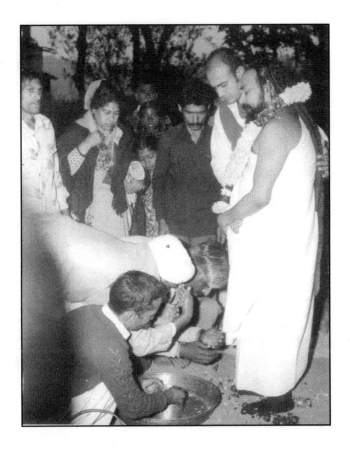

Truth by Your Self and who can lead you towards the experience of Truth is the real Maha Guru. The real Guru would like you to stand on your own feet.

It is the duty of every disciple and devotee to serve the mission of the Guru, so that the world may be benefited with inspiration. It is simply the duty of every disciple to help and serve the Guru, so that the Guru's message can reach everyone in the world. Let all be benefited. As we benefit, it is our duty to help others benefit. The more you go introverted, you feel nearer to the Guru, your Real Self.

Samadhi

Samadhi is when the mind totally gets absorbed into the Real Ultimate Self. The Yogi becomes aware of the Self's existence but without any definitions. Even the earlier imagined, false self's identity also vanishes. This means the thought of 'I' vanishes. In samadhi, a Yogi has no mind, which recognizes or identifies anything. A Yogi simply experiences the Existence, which is Supreme Peace. The relationship between Samadhi and God-Realization functions in this way: in samadhi, the mind has gotten absorbed into the Self. When samadhi occurs, then one regains total Self-Consciousness of Existence. The same thing is recognized as God Realization. Technically it is God-Consciousness. The process is something like a ray of the sun going back to the sun. At the beginning, a bubble of the ocean starts wanting to know what the ocean is, to realize what the ocean is. But that never happens, because the bubble, when away, can never have first hand knowledge (experience) of the ocean. Actually, only consciousness is away and there is no such thing called 'individual soul'. To know what the ocean is, it has to re-enter the ocean. When that happens, it would merge with the ocean, losing its own existence and identification, which was only an imagination. In reality only the ocean exists.

To go into samadhi, one needs total surrender, mentally, in the name of Guru or God. When it happens, the mind ceases to recognize anything else other than Guru. Gradually all imaginations stop. Then the mind stops analyzing or judging anything. This is a very tricky situation. Constant prayers for the granting of surrender help. One has to understand the character of a slave. Just take it as it comes. Firmly take it that it is coming from the Master. The mind always has a tendency to recognize the existence of samsara, spiritually called 'Drishya' meaning scene and 'Shabdha' meaning 'sound'. The mind wants to imagine, define, analyze and judge. All these may be good in this world but when you want the mind to become quiet and go into samadhi, you have to abandon all these during meditation. If the mind understands the Deeksha (initiation) instructions: do not repeat anything and do not imagine; during Dhyana, if any thought or vision or anything occurs, just keep watching and do not try to analyze whether it is good or bad, right or wrong. It is only a purifying process when you try to meditate. The mind is the tape, which has acquired habits and brain acts as tape recorder. When you sit for meditation the mind gets applied onto the brain because of its habits. The purifying process starts when the vasanas (impressions from past experiences) are getting evaporated. Visions and sounds get created by a decoding method from the brain. Then is the time you require enormous patience to allow it to happen. Then you should not analyze or judge what it is, good or bad. Just allow it to happen. Then only the mind can recede, as it has no job to imagine. When the mind recedes, the brain's activation also decreases gradually.

Pray constantly for grace. If the mind surrenders by not trying to analyze anything, its concentration happens. Then automatically it has to get introverted and that is when it is able to touch its origin, inner guide—the Divine Guru. Then Automatic Divine Activity happens and grace starts flowing. Until then you have to put in efforts with dedication, devotion, discipline, and patience—no hurry, no rush, peacefully and tactfully. Moksha, ultimate liberation, is when the mind loses all imaginations, definitions—including identifying the 'I', resolutions and judgments. Once and for all, it gets absorbed into the inner Self. Then you get liberated; you regain consciousness of your real Existence. This is attained by surrender and sadhana (spiritual practice) as explained above. Then there is no rebirth, because rebirth is determined based on the potency and strength of the mind's acquired habits. The mind, if it is less and less violent, more composed, can give an elevated birth, which will further take you towards the Ultimate Truth. If there is no imagination at all, there is no rebirth and you exist, having become one with the Immortal Supreme Soul. The final Samadhi is achieved when the mind totally gets absorbed into the Ultimate Real Self. This is normally recognized as Nirvikalpa Samadhi. The mind is totally free from any imaginations, including 'I', and hence the mind has become one with the Pure Supreme Consciousness of Existence. Once this happens, the mind, which now is Pure Consciousness of Existence, does not go back to body or human consciousness. It is always alert on the Real Self. It does not acquire any further habits, imprints, imaginations, definitions, etc. One has to experience to believe or understand. Thus, even after coming back from Samadhi, the mind is simply Pure Consciousness of Existence. It is a natural Supreme Peace. When a Yogi is talking—even if gossiping or listening to anybody talking, or watching any scene—pure consciousness is totally silent and standstill and does not move or waver, because it does not absorb any further imprints or imaginations.

Pure Consciousness Exists Without
Thoughts And Experiences

We must be clear about the aim of Yoga. The aim of Yoga is to reunite the mind with Pure Consciousness. It is not just to acquire small gifts or powers. To illustrate this we have the story of the great king Bali.

King Bali had won the entire world and established himself as a great emperor, so he began to think, "Now I have won everything, there is nothing left to achieve. Now what will happen to me? Death will occur eventually." In his consciousness, his thoughts were always about 'I' and 'mine'. He approached his Guru, Shukracharya, and prayed to Him to clear his doubts. His Guru answered, "What is the use of me giving you a long talk? I will tell you directly, but you must pay attention closely to what I say. You are consciousness; I am consciousness; this world is also consciousness. When you mind becomes absolutely thoughtless that becomes Pure Consciousness and there is God."

Now King Bali's soul was ripe and so he took his Guru's teaching to heart, and retired into seclusion. "I need to get rid of all my imaginations, and then all that will be left will be Pure Consciousness." So he meditated with concentration and got rid of all the imaginations of his mind and became Self-Realized. He reached that state in which there is no thought of 'I' or 'you', there is simply pure peace.

This is the aim of Yoga. So it is important, while trying to achieve this Truth that you don't have any preconceived ideas of what It is. Then finally the Truth will show itself. This is the basic aim of meditation. The unique method of meditation we teach is that which my Guru, Shivabalayogi, received from the manifestation of Lord Shiva. If we speak of anything, we can only be speaking of our Imaginations. Similarly, on this path people look to find what others' experiences have been. But the experiences are not what are important. Pure Consciousness exists without thoughts and experiences. So whatever the mind tries to visualize, whatever concepts the mind tries to grasp, they actually delay our progress and achievement on this path. Thus on this path we should not get any idea of what it is that we are seeking; we need to experience it. This is like, if you are in a queue for ice cream, but you are given toothpaste. Similarly if you are expecting certain experiences on the path, you may get frustrated or disappointed.

People often ask, "How do we know we are progressing?" My answer is: if your mind is becoming quieter, more still, then you are progressing. If you are getting the consciousness of your existence, then you are progressing. When the mind is constantly creating thoughts and getting excited, it is not going inwards. The mind has so many tricks; it has absorbed so many imprints—all the experiences of this world, all your imaginations, and judgments. All these imprints are absorbed into the mind as acquired habits, called samskaras in spiritual terms. Always the mind has turmoil, imaginations, so it doesn't get into Pure Consciousness.

This meditation is a purification process, but this purification doesn't occur quietly. During the purification, visions and thoughts come. It is just like when you are washing clothes; you see the dirt coming out into the water. In the same way, when the mind is going through the purification, then thoughts and visions occur. But they occur only for a moment, and then they disappear. That is why we need to be so careful in this regard, because if you are watching, then the mind can very easily get involved in the thought, and if it gets involved it can further acquire new imprints. This re-acquiring is so subtle. This is why it is so important not to analyze thoughts during meditation, and this is also why the total cleansing of the mind takes time.

People sometimes ask me, "If we don't analyze, how will it be possible for us to live in this world?" The answer is that living in this world is different from the meditation technique, and yet we find that if we do meditate, then the mind becomes more and more quiet over time, and one can function very effectively in the world. Ultimately we will get rid of all these thoughts and the mind will settle into the Pure Consciousness. Then we will see, as it is said in the Vedas, *Poornam Adah, Poornam Idam*—That Absolute Consciousness outside the creation is Perfect, Whole and Complete; this Creation itself is also Perfect, Whole and Complete. You find when you are dreaming, that the process of dreaming itself is only within your own consciousness. There may be lots of different characters in the dream, and it may appear to occur over a long period of time, years even. You might find that you are yourself one of the characters in the dream, and you might even be aware that you are watching the dream.

This watching consciousness is so easily lost, and when that is lost, then you are unable to see your Real Self. In the same way, this whole world is only within your own consciousness. So you need to practice this meditation, and then you will experience that Absolute. The droplet imagines it is just a droplet. It will be very funny if it imagines it is the ocean. In the same way, this imagined 'I' might try to think it is God, but to really experience the Self, it has to merge into the Self.

Where does the experience of agony in the world come? You see, the mind is habituated to its own thinking. In this audience, some may be happy that I am here, while others may be unhappy that I am here. In the same way, different minds experience this world in different ways. It is not the fault of the world it comes from the mind. You will see that if something bad happens, for those with a good mind, it makes that person unhappy. But for a person whose mind itself is bad, then they feel happy when that bad thing happens. Thus we find that in purifying the mind, first we must get rid of the bad, but then we need to get rid of the good, so that we can go to the Supreme Truth which is beyond these two, good and bad.

My Guru taught both Jnana Marga (Dhyana) and Bhakti Marga, the devotional path. In meditation, one strives to attain a state of no thought, while in Bhakti Marga; one strives to keep one single thought, thinking about God. So we teach the Mrittyuanjaya Mantra, *Om Triayumbakam Yajamahe. . .* which says, "Just as when the pumpkin ripens, then all its seeds are released." In the same way, when this body goes, may my mind go back to God." In Yoga Vasistha, the sage Vasistha instructs Shri Rama, "If you have to think, then think of the Self only." This is called Atma Vicharam.

All of you need to clear the mind of thoughts through meditation. There are many different forms of meditation, but they all aim to achieve single-pointedness of the mind. This technique of meditation taught by my Guru, Shivabalayogi, is the most ancient, and it is not just for single-pointedness. It aims to achieve a state of no-thoughts. When we achieve that state, then the Self is revealed. It is like when Ramana Maharshi started thinking of death when he was a boy. He simply lay down like a dead body, held his breath, and thought, "Am I dead?" He became aware, "No, the consciousness of existence is still present." Even though there were no thoughts, no movement, the Self still existed. This led Him to going into Tapas at Tiruvannamalai.

These agonies of the world, these sufferings are God's gift, which God has given to make us go back to Guru. The mind comes to realize that it is responsible for these sufferings. Initially it will try to blame others, but eventually the wisdom will come, "I am suffering because my mind is weak, because the mind is giving me all these imaginations." If you practice meditation regularly, you will clean this mind. This has always been the basis of religions also, to cleanse the mind. Also they give moral guidance as to how one should behave, because if we are behaving properly, this will give us fewer thoughts also. If the mind is wicked, then it will have thousands of more thoughts. Even if it is weak, but trying to be good, still many thoughts come. The ancient sages describe that the mind will tend to go into one of six basic shapes: extreme greed, extreme anger, extreme attachment to material possessions, extreme stinginess, extreme false pride (ego) and extreme jealousy. Whoever has these, they are the first casualties.

So we should try to have a minimum of good thoughts, just as you drive a car when you want to, and then bring it to a stop when we don't need it. Similarly, we should only think when we need to. There is no need to give up your way of life, no need to go to live in a forest, just settle the mind. For this we need to either have total faith, or we need to completely understand. If we rely on faith, we need to be careful, as the intellect may try to obstruct it. In so many paths, so many great souls have described their experiences on the path, but they said also that we must go beyond these experiences. The true Self is beyond all experiences. In Tapas we saw the need to go within the mind to see the Self. The mind is like a laboratory; you will need to do the experiment. You have to practice; you have to proceed. My Guru said, "Never stop learning." So we try to see the good in people. Even now I try to learn worldly things.

Two Kinds Of Fear

There is a fear and tension in this world which can be overcome by meditation and Bhakti Marga, the path of devotion. This fear has to be overcome. But another type of fear is needed. We must cultivate it. It is not an ordinary worldly fear, but a fear to Guru and fear to God. This fear gets converted into reverence. Only then can you pursue and make progress on the path of spirituality.

A fear like this, the fear of death, made Ramana Maharshi go on the path of sadhana. He pursued that fear and then wanted to overcome it. Thus He became realized. In this way, this same fear of death made me pursue the highest truth. This thought first came to me as a young boy when I heard for the first time the song *Bhaja Govindam* written by Adi Shankaracharya many centuries ago. In the song, He advocates, "Sing the glory of God. Adopt the divine consciousness into your mind, as when death occurs to this physical body, nothing—not your wealth, worldly status or position—nothing is going to save you." Most people do not think of this at all. That is why, when Yudhishthira was asked, "What is the most amazing thing in this world?" He replied, "The most amazing thing in this world is that although every day people everywhere are dying, still nobody thinks it will ever happen to them." Because God's love is universal, He has made death for all.

This so mesmerized my mind, I experienced this fear, and I found I wanted to overcome this problem. I wanted to know, "Is this me, this body which will die?" So this type of fear is needed. But it is not a fear to cause you to panic, to go into a corner and hold your head in despair. We simply need to understand this is the rarest opportunity, the rarest of the rare, to have this human physical body. You need to develop this fear of Guru, of God, and it will become converted into reverence for Guru and God. Then you will be serious in your efforts and use your energy to do the things that are necessary to achieve the goal.

It is like your fear of hunger. Because you have a fear of hunger, you are respectful of it. You are serious in your efforts to earn bread. You don't think, "Oh this is too hard. It's not possible." No, you come to realize the need, so you do it. We never take eating casually. In the same way, death will not wait. It will come when it comes. So the saints have always said to do it now. Put in your efforts now. Don't waste time! Don't waste a precious moment. So this is the importance of this type of fear. This fear needs to be cultivated.

There are two types of ocean—one in which you need to learn to swim and one in which you need to drown. The first ocean is the worldly universe, where we must not drown. We must learn to swim comfortably. We must learn not to get too involved, or it will give you tension and worries. The other ocean you have to drown in is your Real Self. You have to go back to your Real Self, regain that consciousness of who you are really. This is not something you have to learn. Just simply go back to your Real Self.

The Guru Disciple Relationship

(From *His Master's Grace*, recorded at the Dehradun Ashram, 2001)

Our own beloved Guru, Shivabalayogi, always used to tell me the story of Lord Shri Rama, and Lord Hanuman. Just to test our ego, Swamiji used to get annoyed very often. That was His play, His leela. He always used to scold me so many times, even without me doing any faults. For a while, I used to feel bewildered, wondered what wrong have I done my Guru? Yet I used to think in my mind, maybe this is for my benefit; my Guru wants to remove the ego. The Guru wants to remove the prarabdha, the destiny, so that the soul can progress towards the Divine feet of my Satguru. Well, after scolding for a long time, then suddenly He used to ask, "Oh, well now I know that your mind is working in a definite way. It wants to run away from the Guru because the Guru has scolded you. You fool; do you know why I was scolding you? I wanted to remove your prarabdha. Do you understand? I know you want to run away. Look at the devotion the great Hanuman had to His Guru, Lord Shri Rama." Then Swamiji used to tell that beautiful story of the devotion of Hanuman to the Guru and the power of the repetition of the Guru's name.

A legend has it, once all the Devatas and the Sages gathered for a small conference. The matter of discussion was whether Lord Shri Rama's name was more powerful or Shri Rama's bows and arrows are more powerful. It was the time when Lord Rama was ruling the empire of Ayodhya. He had come back after killing the demon King Ravanasura. So thus the matter of discussion turned to these points.

At this, the great Sage Vishvamitra said, "I have seen Lord Rama since His childhood. I know the power of his bows and arrows. I dare to say, even today, if He's tense with his bows and arrows, there is nobody in the universe who can challenge. Well, to this Vasistha says, "Oh, Sage Vishvamitra, and other people who are gathered here, I dare to say, for a disciple a Guru's name is dearer. For a devotee, the Deity's name is dearer. It's more powerful. I say Lord Rama's name is more powerful than His own bows and arrows. Anybody who recites with all devotion, faith, and surrender, Lord Rama's name, even Lord Rama cannot harm them. Anybody who recites the Guru's name with all devotion, faith and surrender, even the Guru, himself, cannot harm him. Such is the power of the Guru's name."

Well, to this Vishvamitra gets annoyed, "Then let us test to this point. Let us see how His devotees fare. So then they selected a person, a king of the Ayodhya Empire, who came under the Ayodhya Empire of Shri Rama. So Vishvamitra goes there to test the person. He selects a particular time when that king, whose name was Chandrabanu, was in meditation, totally absorbed in Dhyana. Due to this, the king could not receive the Sage properly and give him all the reception that was necessary—washing of the holy feet of the Sage, giving him some water, food, shelter, etc. So the king could not attend. Taking this as an excuse, Vishvamitra gets annoyed and immediately goes back from the kingdom. Straight away he reaches Lord Rama, where He was sitting, and complains to Shri Rama that Chandrabanu had disrespected the Sage; he did not receive him properly. At this Shri Rama also gets annoyed and He promises in the name of His bows and arrows, He says, "In the name of my bows and arrows, I promise that tomorrow before sunset, I will kill that person. I will chop off his head." Thus satisfied, Sage Vishvamitra goes away thinking, "Now, let us see how powerful Shri Rama's name is, if that person can recite Shri Rama's name."

Here Sage Narada, who was also in the conference hall of all the Devatas, He comes to that king Chandrabanu. He says, "Chandrabanu, you are a devotee of Lord Rama, but now Lord Rama has promised to Vishvamitra that He will kill you tomorrow before sunset. At this Chandrabanu says, "Now, what shall we do? I love Lord Rama. If He wants, let Him chop off my head. I do not mind. To this Sage Narada says, "Look, that is not the point. In Deva Loka, Vasistha has challenged that Shri Rama's name is more powerful, that devotion to the Guru is more powerful than the Guru himself. You will have to prove this. That is important. Now come, let us go to Lord Hanuman. I will help you at a distance. First, you go to Hanuman, surrender before him, but do not tell who is going to kill you. Just pray for his protection in the name of Lord Rama. Hanuman will be very pleased at Shri Rama's devotees because Hanuman is a great disciple of Lord Rama. He always keeps on reciting Lord Rama's name. So, whoever is a devotee of Lord Rama is always dearer to the great Hanuman. So let us go there."

So, going to that place, first Sage Narada stays at a distance. This king goes and surrenders to Hanuman. After prostrating with due respects and honors, he prays, "Oh, Hanuman, I surrender to you. My life is in danger. I am going to be killed before sunset tomorrow. In the name of the great Lord Rama, the Divine Guru, please protect me." Shri Hanuman was in deep meditation and he came out, started reciting Shri Rama's name, and then said, "Who can kill you? You are a devotee of Lord Rama and you are dearer to me for this reason. I promise in the name of Lord Rama that nobody can kill you tomorrow before sunset. You be here with me. I will protect. The name of our Guru will definitely protect. Come and please stay with me."

So, with his tail Hanuman constructs a small fort-like structure and then makes the king to sit inside. The next day all the Devatas and Sages gather at a distance to see the great Divine play, the leela of Lord Shri Rama and Lord Shri Hanuman. It's between Lord Rama's bows and arrows, and the devotion of a devotee to Lord Rama, the devotion of a disciple to a Guru. Well, as all the armies and Rama's brothers all came, Hanuman was more powerful. He drew them away. Finally Lord Rama himself came in a chariot with all his weapons of bows and arrows. He came and then ordered

Hanuman, "Hanuman, hand over that king to me. I have promised to Sage Vishvamitra that I will kill him before sunset, because this king had disrespected, had dishonored the great Sage. It should not have happened in my empire. I cannot tolerate this."

To this Hanuman says, "My Lord, I love you. With deep love and reverence I prostrate and surrender, but I would like to convey that when Your physical body gets dropped, along with Your physical body, these bows and arrows will also vanish. But for the coming ages, ages after ages, Your name will be eternal and immortal. This name of the Guru, this name of Yours, my Rama, will always protect the devotees. In future ages, when they will learn the marga of devotion they shall recite your name. So I don't want that a Guru's name should be proved that it is not powerful. I want that always a Guru's name is powerful to a devotee. It is more powerful than the Guru himself. So I cannot give this king to you, Sir. Forgive me my Lord."

In the beginning, Lord Rama got enraged and He went on shooting arrows and arrows after arrows. Simply and quietly the great Hanuman stood, repeating the Guru's name "Shri Ram, Shri Ram, Shri Ram, Shri Ram." Nothing happened to Hanuman. Those arrows, which were shot by the bow of Shri Rama, by Shri Rama Himself, they could not harm Hanuman at all. They all fell at a distance. They merged into the body of Lord Hanuman, it is said. So that, finally all the Devatas and Sages came to Lord Rama and prayed to Him, "This we wanted to test the power of a Guru's name, our Lord, so that has been proved today. Really, devotion is more powerful than the Deity Itself." So that's all. The Devatas and Sages, they went away satisfied, and Shri Rama was very happy with Lord Hanuman and King Chandrabanu, who was a great devotee of Lord Hanuman.

So Swamiji always used to tell these stories to me very often. "Look, even when Lord Rama wanted to kill Hanuman, Hanuman did not sacrifice the devotion to His Guru, to Rama." So even if a Guru wants to harm and test you, put you into examination, you should not sacrifice the devotion to the Guru because this devotion and repetition of the Guru's name will always help you, protect you from all evils and harmfulness. The Guru is bound to protect you always. So, like this, Swamiji used to tell the story of Hanuman and Shri Rama.

A Guru is a torchbearer to a sadhak, a disciple. Guru always inspires a disciple because a disciple, a human being, is always likely to become careless and not pursue on the path of spirituality seriously. He or she is likely to lose heart, because on the serious journey of Tapas spirituality, the sadhana is not really easy. However, if one can obtain the blessings of the Guru, who is the ocean of kindness, it will become easier for a disciple to go on the path of sadhana, Tapas.

I would like to recount one of my experiences during my Tapas. For the last four months, when I was asked to invoke Lord Shiva and Parvati for darshan and blessings, as ordained by my Guru, Shivabalayogi, I invoked. In the end, when I was in deep samadhi, I suppose, they woke me up. For a while I could not understand who were standing, dazzling and glowing, which is inexplicable. You cannot just explain. It's impossible. You cannot reproduce. Such is the appearance. My mind was totally absorbed into it. Well, with a great smile and affection, they spoke, "Now you have become a Yogi, my Child. Blessed you are that your Guru had blessed you. However, now that we have come in front of you, you do not require your Guru anymore. You can ask for any boon. We can give you all the powers. You will achieve name and fame on this earth and we will give you a long life."

Spontaneously it came to me, I said, "I want my Guru, I love. I don't want a long life on this earth, my Lord. I don't want any name, fame or any power. I don't want anything. I just want to be at the lotus feet of my Guru. I want Him. I want everything through my Guru only. I want to serve in His mission. Please, grant me the boon that my devotion to my Guru shall not diminish, shall not vanish, forever. Please bless me for this."

The Divine Lord was very much pleased. He blessed and spoke many other things and He gave me the blessings, so that the Guru's protection will always be there. And then they vanished. Such is the power of Guru. You see, when the Divine appears before you, you cannot cheat the Divine. I promise. It is not possible. Whatever devotion you are used to, such a thing will come out spontaneously. You cannot think, plan and say. If you are really, really devoted to the Guru, and if you are used to the Guru's devotion, spontaneously such a thing will come out, that you want the Guru. So that's when the Lord, before giving you the final samadhi, will test you for the ahamkara, for that ego, whether you love your Guru, whether when you come out of the non-duality, whether you will behave properly. It is always tested. You see, our own Shivabalayogi, He never claimed Himself to be Lord Shiva or Goddess Parvati though He was the formation of Ardhanarishwara—Lord Shiva and Goddess Parvati. But He always said that Lord Shiva is His Guru. Shivabalayogi, our beloved Guru, worshiped Lord Shiva all the time. Even when sometimes we wanted to call Him Shivabala Yogishwara, the Gurudev asked us not to call Him Shivabala Yogishwara, because He said, "It's only Lord Shiva who is the Yogishwara, the Ishwara, the Lord of all the Yogis. You can call me Shivabalayogendra."

So imagine, how can we call ourselves as the gurus? We are at the lotus feet of our Divine Guru, Shivabalayogi. We will have to behave the way our Guru taught us. We will have to worship Shivabalayogi. When it is in Nirvikalpa Samadhi, in the Advaita, the non-duality, only one single Self, the Divine, the Shivabalayogi, the Guru, exists. I do not exist at all. But when we come out of the samadhi, then we have to behave on this earth, we will have to inspire others, show the right path, the right behavior. In duality, Shivabalayogi is my Lord, my Guru. Shivarudra Balayogi is the Lord's disciple, child, and servant. The place is at the lotus feet of the Divine Guru. I really do not know whether we are eligible to sit at His lotus feet at all. We do pray to the great Divine Guru, Shivabalayogi, to grant us surrender, grant us the boon to sit at His lotus feet and work on the mission.

Swamiji used to say, "If I smile at you, that means I will give you all the worldly help, wealth and benefits, everything. If I get annoyed with you, remember I will give you the boon. I will take you out of the bondage of the samsara. I will give you the boon of enlightenment, the liberation totally". I used to say, "Swamiji, your scoldings are your teachings to me. Your beatings are blessings and boons. I am sure you will take me out of the bondage of this world." Swamiji used to say, "Take my beatings and scolding. Then the world cannot beat you."

As a student it is your duty to acquire knowledge and wisdom. It's your duty to do sadhana. It is your duty to undertake meditation. Because when you become masters, when you have become well educated, you can educate others also. You can definitely help others. That is the path of the dharma, your duty. So when you have become an enlightened soul, then you can definitely help others. But remember, undertaking meditation is certainly not selfishness. Some people have asked me also, whether meditation is hypnotizing oneself. Is it not that you are going to hypnotize your own self? I say certainly it is not so. Your mind's imagination is bondage. You have hypnotized yourself by thinking, defining everything as the mind has willed it. Thus you have hypnotized yourself. So, the world is sitting in your mind. By meditating you are trying to liberate yourself. In fact, if you meditate perfectly, you will be liberating yourself from the hypnotizing efforts of your mental imaginations.

Every imagination of the mind is bondage, illusion. Because the mind recognizes, it analyzes, it judges, it comes to a conclusion, and that thing sits in the mind. Then the mind thinks that as the real one. But the truth can be something else. That's why, in meditation, when you are initiated, you are told not to imagine anything. The truth can be something else. And that is also the reason, when many people keep asking me, "I have been meditating for so many years and I have not yet obtained any experience. I have not obtained any lights." Nothing is required. Experiences do not mean that you are going to have visions, lights or currents. The actual experience in meditation is that, if the mind shall start losing all the imaginations, it shall stop absorbing the worldly things from the universe.

You see it is, after all, the brain that has given you the consciousness of this universe. When I address you as 'You', it is

Soul—You, the Immortal Soul. The brain is an organ in this body. It is in touch with the universe through the nervous system and sensory organs: the eyes, nose, ears, touch, smell, taste, and so on. Through this process, the brain receives all the messages, and vice versa. It sends orders back. During this process, the brain reflects. When it reflects and it is active, the mind is attracted to the brain. The mind is your conscious energy, the soul's consciousness. The mind gets applied on the brain and the brain, in turn, gets activated more and more. So in the process, a type of circling takes place, just like a hen coming out of an egg and the egg coming out of the hen. The circle goes on, goes on and a never-ending illusionary process takes place. So the mind catches the illusionary reflections of the brain, and in the process, it takes the shape of the same imaginations and it runs and runs.

It is just like this, you are watching a movie. Biologically, technically in any way, you are not at all involved with the movie. It's only a cinema that's going on the screen. You are watching. But gradually as you go on watching, your concentration gets sucked into it. Thus your mind, your consciousness also gets sucked into it and you start imagining yourself in the movie. You start imagining all the happiness and unhappiness, everything that happens in the movie, as your own. Gradually you forget that you have been watching a movie. You experience everything and you start thinking that you are experiencing everything. Thus an illusion starts and you forget. A long illusion starts. In the same way, mysteriously and peculiarly, the soul's consciousness, after watching the movie of the world, has gotten involved mentally.

Well, it is ultimately a mystery, whether the hen came first or the egg came first, whether the energy of the Divine wired the brain up like this. This you experience only in samadhi that everything came from the Divine, the Ultimate Truth that simply exists as an all-pervading Spirit—the energetic, Supreme Consciousness. However, this cannot be simply explained and told through theories. This cannot be demonstrated. An individual will have to experience. So thus the mind gets hypnotized. Now the sadhana, meditation, is taught so that the soul can liberate itself from the effects of this illusion. Gradually you are taught to control the mind. Seeing the technique of meditation, unknown to you, your consciousness is getting turned back to your own Self. Thus you are trying to go back to the Self.

Our Beloved Satguru, Shivabalayogi, Shri Swamiji always used to keep teaching through silence and occasionally through a few words. In 1978, when He came to Dehradun, He called me one day and started talking, "Look, there is a mentally handicapped boy in Mysore. He's very violent to his kith and kin. I have told them that he would be all right if he comes and stays at the ashram. I told them I will talk to you, Seenu, for that you would love to serve him, whether you would like to keep him here and look after him." Such was the beautiful way of Swamiji talking. I have already told, He never spoke authoritatively. He never ordered, "But you will have to do this one. You must do this one!" Very sweetly, just like a mother and father, just like a friend, He used to call us, and then He used to ask for our willingness. "I thought of bringing him here, if you are willing to look after him." Thus Swamiji spoke always very sweetly and beautifully.

Thus from my side there was no question of disregarding the Guru's orders. Whatever He wanted me to do, that was a boon from the Guru. For me, that was tapas. That was my sadhana always. That was a thing which could remove my ego—the imagination of the individual self—and which could lead me to the lotus feet of the Guru, the Divine all- pervading Spirit. I readily said, "Yes Swamiji, whatever you want me to do, please order. I would love to do it. That is my Tapas." Swamiji was very pleased and He smiled and He told a story, "Look, a person who listens to the Guru's orders is always benefited. Nobody can harm such a person. Even the bad and the worst things get converted into sadhana for such a person. It becomes the best sweets for him, the prasadam. Even the worst decayed things also get converted into beautiful sweets and get converted into prasadam." Then He told me the story.

In olden days, the Gurus used to go on trekking for long distances. The whole day they used to keep walking. In the evening they used to camp on the outskirts of a particular town or village. And then they used to send the devotees, disciples, to go inside the village and to bring bhikshu, the alms. They used to go and seek food through alms, bhikshana. Then they used to bring that food, offer it to the Guru first. After the Guru partook of the food, then the disciples used to have it as prasadam. Once the Guru wanted to test his disciples. He went on walking for several days. He never stopped at any village. He never camped. He never stopped even for a moment. He went on walking. The devotees, the disciples were quite exhausted. They were terribly hungry. But they were too scared to talk to the Guru, to ask and inform the Guru that they were hungry. They kept quiet. So after walking for seven days, on the eighth day, the Guru was walking through a deep thick forest, a jungle. There he saw a dog had died and the body had decayed. A foul smell was coming out of the body, so that the disciples closed their nose. They thought, "Oh God, this is too bad a smell." The Guru ordered them, "Look, I know you are already hungry, my sweet children. I want you all to eat this dog. Now come on and get it." The disciples felt very bad. They moved away. "Oh, this is very bad. This is giving a very bad, foul smell. We cannot eat such things. It is not possible." They kept away.

One of the disciples had the wisdom. He said, "There must be some secret if the Guru has ordered. He wants to give me some boon. He wants to give me some sadhana." Without any questions, the disciple straight away went to the dog, and he put his hands onto it. He wanted to eat and started eating. As he put his hands and went on eating, it all got converted into beautiful sweets. He went on eating and he ate his stomach full. He felt very satisfied of the Guru's prasad. Then they started walking while the other disciples felt very bad. "Oh God, look at him. He listened to the Guru's orders and he got. We should have listened to the Guru's orders. Oh, we are egotistic. We did not listen to the Guru's orders. That's why we did not get anything. Well, next time we must listen to the Guru's orders, and instantly do as he wants us to do," so they all decided.

The Guru smiled, because he knew they were still egotistic. They didn't have that temperament of surrender to the Guru. Well, they went on walking for another few days. The next time the Guru stopped on the outskirts of a village, he said to the disciples, "Look on the tree there, there is a ghost." Swamiji used to call it 'brahma bhotam'. "That's a ghost which had a curse in its previous life, so it is living there. It is waiting for me to come here. I want to liberate that ghost from that life. So, go and bring that ghost."

So the disciples thought, "Well, the Guru has ordered." So everybody started saying, "I will go first, I will go first." They quarreled. Finally, one by one they went. The ghost was very powerful. It threw them from the tree, and drew them away. All the disciples came back depressed. "Look, we tried to obey the Guru's orders. Even then we are not blessed. That means the Guru is partial. He blessed only that disciple, but why did not he bless us?" They started thinking and doubting Guru's blessings like that, because they had egos. So they had doubts. Their minds were not clear. It was not pure. Their hearts, *antah karanam*, their heart and mind were not pure.

So this disciple who had obeyed the Guru's orders previously, and who took the prasadam of the decayed dog, he comes to the Guru. "Tell, my Lord, because you have ordered, I would like to obey and bring the ghost to you. But before going, I want to take your special blessings, because the ghost might harm me. Please give me the technique, how to bring the ghost and make it surrender to you." The Guru was pleased and he said, "Okay, you are the right disciple. You have wisdom. Now, I want you to go and bring the ghost. Go first, talk to the ghost as a friend. Quietly and sweetly, try to go nearer, and suddenly catch hold of the hairs of the ghost. Then the ghost cannot do anything. It will simply surrender and come here." So listening to Guru's orders and his technical instructions, the disciple went to the ghost, and in the same way as taught by his Guru, the ghost was brought to surrender. Finally the Guru liberated the ghost from its life of the curse.

Swamiji narrated this story on that day in 1978. Even today it rings in my ear so beautifully as taught by my Guru. Well I prostrated and said, "I would love to serve my Guru's orders." In the same way I prayed, "Swamiji, you please bless me so that I will be able to look after that mentally handicapped boy. Please bless so that he does not become violent and listens to me." Swamiji was very much pleased. He blessed me. He gave me a small piece of vibhuti, and said, "Because you have faith in Guru, you will be successful in looking after him. Do not worry. You go ahead. Then I will send him here."

Well, in the same year, that mentally handicapped boy came to me and he stayed for thirteen years, until he died of some hemorrhage in 1991. From 1978 to 1991, he stayed with me. Swamiji's blessings worked wonderfully. The boy was very sweet. During the beginning, he tried to be violent. Then I used to talk to him, pacify him. I used to look after him. He became so much attached to me. When I used to scold him, sometimes when he used to trouble me, I used to tell him, "Now look, I'm going to send you away to Mysore. You are not a good boy. You are not going to stay with me." Imagine that mentally handicapped boy, one day he cried. He cried and started telling he doesn't want to go anywhere. He doesn't want to go away from me. He said, "No, I want to stay with you. I won't go away." I was very much moved. Such was the blessings of the Divine Guru, Shivabalayogi. And that boy, I taught him to put water in the garden, pour water to the plants in the garden. He learned how to lock and unlock the gate, and he used to dust. I wanted him to help me in bhajans also. I used to give him something to do harmony on. Then I used to sing with my dholak (drum). So like that, he lived with me for thirteen years.

There's the story of another boy who also came from Andra Pradesh. After this success, then some other devotee, whose brother was also mentally handicapped, had come for Swamiji's blessings. Swamiji said, "I will send this boy to Dehradun and Seenu will look after very affectionately." And then Swamiji told me that, "I will be bringing one more boy. Is it alright?" I said, "Well, Swamiji, it is alright. I don't mind. Please kindly bless me, so that I'll be able to look after him." So that boy also came. But he did not live for very long. I think that is also a play of the Divine Guru. He was destined to come and live in the ashram during the last days. He lived only for six months. He used to get epileptic fits also.

Finally Swamiji, later on He explained, that boy also had been cursed, due to his misbehavior to women in his previous life. So he had become like that in this life. This boy always used to keep shouting in such a matter, very filthily always. He used to run away. Then I had to go after him, bring him again and again. It was so difficult to keep him. However, we tried to look after him in the best way. Then later on, after he died, Swamiji said, "I wanted him to come and serve in this ashram, stay here with you, Seenu, because you are a noble soul. I thought that his curse will be wiped out. He will be blessed with a lovely human life in his next, so that he can do more sadhana. Thus I wanted him to be here. Even though I knew that he would not live for very long." Well, after he came, he lived for some time. He used to soil the whole room, on his body, and being very unclean. Whatever he used to eat, he used to vomit twice or thrice in a day. So I had to wash his body totally. I had to clean the soil. The sweepers would not like to do such work. Well, what happened, some devotees who loved me, out of too much love to me, went to Swamiji. They spoke to Him, "Swamiji, Seenu should not be made to work like this. It is very bad. He comes from a very good family background. Why is he made to clean the soil?" Then Swamiji told them, "Look, do not interfere. Seenu is doing this because I asked him to do it, to obey me. Out of his sheer love and devotion to the Guru, he is doing. Let him do this. His prarabdha, destiny, will be wiped out very soon, and in due course of time he will be able to do Tapas. He will get the Tapas Phala, the fruit of Tapas. So do not interfere." Thus, Swamiji had blessed me in this way.

In the Guru Gita it is said, "There is no reality beyond Guru. There is no penance beyond Guru. There is no knowledge beyond Guru. With total surrender, prostrations to that Guru. The form of Guru is the root of meditation. The feet of Guru are the root of worship. The teaching of the Guru is the root of all mantras. The grace of the Guru is the root of salvation, enlightenment. The Guru is pure, with a peaceful, good nature, speaking very little, conveying the message through silence, devoid of all passions and anger. The Guru, the one who is of righteous conduct and self control, is the real Guru. I prostrate with full surrender to such a Guru."

So, always surrender to the Guru. Do not abandon the initiation, the sadhana that which the Guru has given to you. Surrender with complete faith, unquestionably. Surrender to the Guru, always unconditionally, and you shall become liberated and enlightened. Surrender in such a way, even if the Guru tests, even if the Guru wants to disturb you, the mental surrender shall be unwavering, so that no power of the universe can disturb. Never get confused. You should never sit with such people who are likely to confuse your devotion, your faith to the Guru. Abandon such people's company. Always have the company of good people. Be in touch with such people who talk about the Guru and the Guru's greatness, who are really the gems of the Guru's disciples. Talk to such people always, who always talk about the Guru, who always can remove your doubts, who can inspire you, give you the total faith and surrender towards the Guru. Only be in the company of such people.

The seven crores of great mantras are all for the bewilderment and disturbance of the mind. There is only one great mantra: the two lettered word 'gu'-'ru', the one who dispels the darkness of ignorance—Guru. Oh noble, divine soul, first listen to the teaching of the Guru. You will be the real blessed, if you can sit in front of the Guru and listen to Him. After that, reflect upon it in your mind. If your mind has really absorbed what the Guru has taught you, if your mental concentration was total when the Guru was teaching, and your mind has absorbed it, this is the second state. The third one is when you put that into practice, the sadhana, the real meditation. This type of profound meditation becomes the cause of complete, full knowledge, wisdom, liberation and enlightenment.

Every sadhana as taught by the great, liberated, enlightened Gurus, is equally important. People of this world, the devotees who really want to do sadhana, should shun criticizing others' sadhana. It is very natural for the devotees to propagate the teachings of their Guru. But at the same time, remember, do not try to judge or condemn other Guru's teachings. Do not try to analyze. Just go ahead with the sadhana; because you are simply wasting your energies, your time, and thus you are unable to do sadhana. My Guru, Shivabalayogi, told a story about this also, how that by paying too much attention to others' faults, too much attention to others, on criticizing others, you hardly have any time to do sadhana for your own self.

Once upon a time, there lived a Saint who was doing Tapas. In the town the king had constructed him a small ashram, and the monk was living there, who was trying to do sadhana. It so happened after some time, the king had given some land to a prostitute, who constructed a home for herself and who started living there. At this, the monk got disturbed. He started thinking, "Oh God, how bad this lady is. She's a prostitute. She always does bad karmas. Why has she come and stayed here?"

Every day, people used to visit her. This monk, coming out of his room, used to keep watching. For every person who visited that prostitute, he used to count, "Oh, now she has done one bad karma." The monk used to keep a stone for each karma. Every day he used to count like this and put a stone, and those stones gradually, in due course of time, became a small mountain. So he used to think, "So much of bad karma this woman has done. My God, how can she get liberated? She will go to the hell always." So thus, always he used to keep thinking about that prostitute only, and her bad karma. He used to keep counting that.

On the other hand, what happened to the prostitute? One day suddenly she saw the monk standing in the compound of his ashram. When she saw him, she was very much pleased. Her mind became very peaceful. She was satisfied at the darshan of a saint, a monk. She thought, "How beautiful. How fortunate I am, that being a prostitute and a doer of sins, I have been blessed with the darshan of a monk." Then she painted a picture of that monk, kept it in her puja room, and started worshiping the monk. Though her karmas were bad, her mind always was on the monk. She had accepted the monk as a Guru, as God, as Divine. She had started worshiping and doing meditation on the form of the Guru. Thus, throughout her life she spent her time worshiping the monk.

So, in the end, both of them died. The prostitute also died, and the monk also died. To take the prostitute, God's servants came. They said, "Now you are liberated. We will be taking you to the Moksha—to the Parama Pada, the Supreme Abode of the Divine. Whereas the monk was to be sent back to the earth to be born as an animal. To this the monk resented. "Why this discrimination? All along my life I was doing sadhana. I had accepted the life in a monastery. I was a monk, I was a sannyasi." To this the servants of the God of Death said, "Look, throughout your life, though you had adorned the cloth of the monk, though you were living in an ashram, your mind was always on the bad karma. It was sinning all the time. It was trying to judge and condemn that woman. Whereas that woman, though her karmas were sin, all along her life, her mind was worshiping you as a Guru—worshiping the monk as the Divine. So thus, her heart and mind had become pure. She had attained a state of samadhi, and she became eligible to get liberated."

So telling this, Swamiji always used to say, "Look out for your mind. It is very important. Do not waste your energies by trying to criticize others, by trying to find faults with others sadhana. Do your own sadhana. Concentrate all your energies, your mind, your consciousness, everything on your own sadhana in priority. Totally, just be preoccupied so that you don't have time to find faults with others." That was how Swamiji taught us always, in such a way. He always used to advise us, "Whenever anything happens, whenever you feel sad, whenever you feel depressed, first try to think where you are at fault. Try to find out what is your weakness and try to rectify your weakness. Try to do more meditation. Do sadhana. Then your mind's depression, your mind's faults, everything will get rectified, and your soul will get elevated towards liberation and enlightenment."

Ultimately, that was how Swamiji always taught and advised us. It was such a beautiful experience. Twenty years of physical experiences with Swamiji is really very inexplicable. It is not possible to explain everything with these few words. However, I have tried to talk a little bit, whatever that was possible. I hope the devotees who listen to this will be benefited in their sadhana, in their devotion to the Guru. Swamiji always used to say, "Surrender to the Guru unconditionally." So thus, we will have to surrender unconditionally to the lotus feet of the Guru and in the name of Guru. Come and chant with me, *Om Shivaya Shivabalayogendraya Parabrahmanaya.*

PART TWO

TALKING WITH BABA
Answers to Spiritual Questions of Devotees and Sadhaks

Questions From A Student Of
The Upanishads And Bhagavad-Gita

BABA:

The study of the Upanishads is called Brahma Vidya, the Science of Ultimate Truth. It is said that each of the Upanishads contains a statement of the goal of life and a description of the way to reach that goal. Vedanta is based on the direct experiences of the Seers of Truth. Their conclusion is that the Divine is within the human and that humans may succeed in recognizing the Divine within themselves by removing misunderstandings about our own identity. Truth is all-pervading. We need not go here and there to find it. All effective scriptures and sadhana lead us to our own Self. By looking ever more deeply into our own Being, through meditation, we may come face to face with what we have been seeking and thereby come to rest. For most, this takes time and a long-term commitment to our chosen sadhana.

Questioner:

Our Upanishads and the Advaita Vedanta of Shri Shankara seem to explain that the Supreme is the Atman in the physical body?

BABA:

It is true. The basic clue is the mind. Its nature is Pure Consciousness and peace. See how infinite is the mind itself, no particular form. You cannot catch hold of it and show it to anybody, as 'this is the mind'. Only based on thoughts, you say, "My mind wants to eat or sleep." Sometimes you might say, "I want to," but actually it is the mind's imagination. This mind's ultimate origin is the Divine. Just like the sun's ray is to the sun, the mind is to God. This is not only in humans, but also in all creatures and substances. The difference is in the manifestation. This Ultimate Truth is Supreme Consciousness which is all-pervading. A Yogi experiences the Self's existence in Nirvikalpa Samadhi. There will not be an iota of imagination, not even the thought of 'I' or 'Existence', but you experience the existence. You become aware of your existence as Atman. A Yogi remains there effortlessly with contentment.

As long as there is an imagination that you are a devotee, your God also exists in your mind. In all religions of the universe, all types of sadhanas, rituals of worship and prayers were recommended by the founders, so that you can make your ever wandering mind single-pointed with concentration. See, the mind is always brooding about the past or is anxious about the future, whereas both do not exist, actually, except in your imagination. When the mind gradually loses all its imaginations, it starts going introverted. Meditation means 'attention to'. When the mind is wandering, its attention is towards the world, and hence it has no time to notice or be aware of itself. When the mind goes introverted, it gets a chance to become aware of its Real Self. When it becomes one with the Supreme Self, this is recognized as God. But actually when you reach that, you would have lost the earlier imagination of 'I'—there is no Seer and no Seen.

Questioner:

In the Bhagavad-Gita, Lord Krishna teaches Arjuna that he should totally surrender to Him and leave the fruits of all actions. What is this principle? Again in His Viswarupa, Lord Krishna shows that He is in everything and everything is in Him. Is it a simultaneous merger of the Self and the Supreme?

BABA:

The principle of surrender and detachment from the fruits of all actions is connected to the mind. If you surrender and do not bother about the results, this means that the mind is becoming quiet. It is abandoning all imaginations of analyzations and judgments. This is also not easy, unless you are 100 percent devoted to God with love. Remember that in Bhakti Marga (the path of devotion) it is taught to take things as they come, by considering, "Let it happen as you wish, my Lord." The idea is that the mind shall not go into agitations. See, what Krishna says, you do karma (actions) and the results are automatic. They may be favoring you or they may not be. Unless your mind is able to accept this, it will have no peace and will go into agitations. Agitations of the mind mean, for instance, brooding, dislike, hard feelings, having grudges and so on. Whoever has these feelings, such a person's mind is the first casualty. In addition, such a person may become dangerous to others. The mind takes shapes according to extreme feelings. These shapes are divided into six names: Kama (greed), Krodha (extreme anger), Lobha (extreme stinginess or meanness), Moha (extreme attachment to the materialistic world), Madha (false pride, arrogance), Matsarya (jealousy). Whoever has these things in their minds are the first casualties. Gradually one is able to abandon all these things and rise step by step towards Self-Realization. The mind has no third way. Either it has to wander aimlessly like a monkey in this world, due to imaginations and judgments, or, when it is able to leave all imaginations, it goes introverted towards the Divine. Thus, simultaneously, the imagined self of the mind merges with the real Eternal Supreme Self.

Questioner:

In the *Mahabharata*, at the end there is a chapter dealing with the final journey of the Pandavas to heaven with a faithful dog (named Dharma). One by one they fall behind, and in the end only Yudhishthira and the dog reach heaven. What is the concept of Self-Realization here?

BABA:

The dog accompanying Yudhishthira means simply, only the

acquired habits of your mind go with you. Faithfully like a dog, these are the only things that go wherever you go, even after death, whether they are good or bad. Here Dharma is explained as such good habits of the mind, acquired through good karmas. They go with you when the physical body gets dropped. None of the kith and kin go, no matter how much dearer they are. Throughout his life, Yudhishthira had followed the path of dharma in the worldly life. Here, I mean the upholding of moral values. For Self-Realization, you are required to undertake such sadhana as to abandon all imaginations of the mind, make it rise above the dualities of good and bad. This is Spiritual Dharma. The other one is Physical Dharma, undertaking such care and sadhana, so as to keep your body as healthy as possible. Here dharma means your duty in its highest pitch. These three things combined: physical health, mental health and moral health are actually religion. If you are able to practice all three to their perfection, only then you are a perfect religious person. The rest is rubbish and selfishness.

Yudhishthira had some guilt that he had lied during the war and that became the basic reason for the killing of Guru Drona. But it was actually not so. Always the purpose is more important than whether you are telling a lie or the truth. If it is for a larger cause, for the benefit of the entire society or humanity, such a lie told for the benefit of the entire humanity comes to be known as Dharma. Another place where Yudhishthira failed to uphold dharma was during Draupadi's disrobing episode. Yudhishthira thought, as he had lost his wife in the gamble, he had no right to protest when Draupadi was supposed to be disrobed. If not as his wife, he could have considered her at least a woman who needed protection. He could have protested, as there was no such agreement that the Kauravas would disrobe her, if lost in the gamble. The Kauravas had no business to do so. Here what he considered Dharma was for his selfish honor.

In the end it is written that Yudhishthira had to go through hell. The vision was the play of his mind's imaginations. Even a slightest feeling of guilt can make you see such visions and have such experiences in the next life. The other brothers and Draupadi fell earlier because of their own egos and the acquired habits of their minds. There is mention of heaven for Yudhishthira and not liberation or Self-Realization, so it is really difficult to judge whether he was Self- Realized or not. He was a great Dharmatma in this world, no doubt. There is more in these episodes, but I think this much is enough to understand the philosophy of mind and its acquired habits.

Questioner:

With all his knowledge of the Self acquired through Gita, what happens to Arjuna's Self- Realization in the end?

BABA:

There is a difference between knowledge acquired through discourse and the knowledge experienced through sadhana. Such a mighty soul Arjuna was, but often he fell into depressions caused by misunderstandings about dharma. There is no mention of Arjuna becoming Self-Realized. It is difficult to judge. He was a great devotee of Lord Krishna, but also showed a desire for selfish honor rather than for the larger cause of dharma. Self-Realization is very rare. Lord Krishna says, "Arjuna, more than anybody else, like a Tapasvi, person of karma, etc., the Yogi is dearer to me. So become a Yogi. The Yogi is the only one who has lost all imaginations of the mind and allowed the mind to merge with the Supreme Self."

Questioner:

As soon as a child is born, under the total nursing care of the parents, both mentally and physically, the child has apparently no capability of its own. The samskara of the soul is the bestowed destiny of the child, both mentally and physically, is yet to take place. Going by the perceptions of the Upanishads and teachings of Bhagavad-Gita, where are these samskara, destiny, etc. of the person until they actually take effect in one's life? If they are again linked to the thought processes of the individual, as and when the individual's mind and body develop, how are the effects regulated until such time?

BABA:

After the birth, until such time as the brain develops to receive the world's reflections, all the samskaras (acquired habits of the mind) remain recorded in the mind. The mind exists as long as there are definitions born out of imaginations. If there were no thought samskaras, the mind would not be able to exist. The illusion would have come to an end, with the mind merging with the Real Self, the Ultimate Truth. The mind itself cannot remain without a gross body. The mind is like a tape with all its recordings and the brain acts as tape player and recorder. Though until this time, humanity has not been able to obtain a conclusive answer as to which came into existence first. In my experience and opinion, I would say that both mind and brain came into existence together, simultaneously. Here, when I talk about the brain, I do not mean human beings only. All creatures have something like a brain, which experts of that particular field may name and define in different ways. The brain enables all creatures to be in touch with this universe. Both are there because of each other. Without the mind using it, the brain would die. Without the brain, the mind cannot come in touch with the world. As long as the mind has not become quiet, it cannot go back to the Self. When there are thoughts, only then it is known as 'mind'. It does not exist without a gross body.

Questioner:

The parents bring up the child and an integrated mental and physical development of the child starts taking shape. Even though all babies (in one home) are brought up in similar ways, depending on the samskara of the particular soul, each baby is different from the other. One may be very quiet. Another may be always crying, one docile, the other extremely active, etc. This may, to a great extent, influence the shaping of the person's future. Next as the child grows into an adult, both mental and physical faculties develop. Here again in rating the person, either the mental or physical capabilities become the over riding factor. For example, somebody may be very intelligent but physically very weak. Somebody may be physically very healthy, strong and aggressive but mentally very poor. Somebody may be balanced in both. Somebody's mind may be kind, somebody's may be spiritually oriented, somebody's may be materially oriented, somebody's cruel, etc. As a result, a person's overall performance and achievements in life will apparently depend on the stronger of the two (mental or physical) or a balanced one that is a result of the combination. Ultimately the person is termed as good, bad, honest, strong, weak, shrewd, wise, pious, foolish, etc.

BABA:

Yes, each baby is different because it is carrying habits acquired already, perhaps in previous lives. Based on the strength of intensity of the mind's thoughts, a basic nature builds up. Everything depends mostly on this basic nature. The world is the same and is in its place, but every human mind has taken the imprint according to its own mental perceptions. The poet has one understanding, the scientist has another. A spiritual teacher, one who is a scholar and has read scriptures but not experienced the Truth, has his own. When you actually become a Realized Soul, there is no such understanding at all. No jumping to any conclusions. Simply remain in the Real Self. That is why ancient Rishis used the word Anantham, meaning: no end, no conclusions. A sadhak is taught not to bother too much about understanding beyond a point, because you will simply keep your mind in existence by trying to understand, and thereby going back consciously to the Ultimate Truth, the Self would be elusive. Even in Tapas also, one is able to observe only up to a point, because when the mind gets totally, 100 percent concentrated, remaining quiet by practice, then, as it starts going towards samadhi, the mind gets de-linked from intelligence. You can locate your Real Self, but you cannot observe anything. One simply becomes aware of one's existence, no 'I', no 'You', no devotee, no God, no seer and no scene.

As long as Realization does not occur through practice, the mind is in existence, carrying habits and constantly acquiring new habits. Through the sensory organs, when matter's existence is transmitted to the brain, the brain recognizes, analyses, judges, and in the process acquires imprints into the mind. This is the problem. Birth after birth, it is carried until the time is ripe and mind is able to recognize its own fault, until the mind tries, learns, and practices to remain quiet.

This sadhana, such as meditation and others, is taught in religions. Through practice, the mind has gone out of control, and through practice, it has to become quiet. Then Mano Laya, the receding of the mind, happens—consciousness going back to the Self. Detachment from the world is necessary for the mind. Until then it does not get liberated. It is born again, and dies again. *Punarapi Jananam Punarapi Maranam*, meaning good and bad, and so on are dualities of the world. One is important because of the other. By sadhana, you raise your mind from these dualities to enable it to go back to the Self, and remain there eternally, peacefully, totally contented with the Self—Anantham, no end.

Questioner:

In all these cases, is mind still the governing factor? If so, how does the mind control and regulate the physical growth and development of the person also?

BABA:

Mind is only a small spark of the Ultimate Self, the Divine. This Divine energy is the governing factor. I am answering as Divine energy, because directly the Divine has no extrovert consciousness. It is always in Mahasamadhi, introvert and in itself. However, with an Automatic Divine Activity, the Divine energy governs. See, the mind, itself, cannot do anything without the availability of another existence, such as oxygen, and so on. Energy is working everywhere. At some places it may appear active to naked eyes, and at some places it may appear inert. Very often energy exists like the sweetness in sugar, butter in the milk. A small spark of the mind itself will be helpless, without availability of other forms of energy. As the Self inspires the mind, the same Self is everywhere and its energy is flowing. In both death and birth, there is energy. In good and bad, there is energy. Based on these observations and experiences in Tapas, the Ultimate Self that is recognized as the Divine is the governing factor. Along with effort, which is inspired by the energetic consciousness of the mind, luck also has to favor the sadhak to achieve anything in this world. Some call this as God's grace; some call it as luck favoring, and so on, but the energy is the same. This is not the sankalpa (the wish) of God. It is just happening. By trying to be as careful as possible, practice thinking progressively. Be in the company of the good, the wise, the learned and experienced. Before death shall occur to the physical body, try making the mind quiet. Simultaneously, it becomes pure, peaceful, and contented. This is what is required in priority.

Punarapi jananam punarapi maranam punarapi janani jathare chayanam iha samsare bahu dustare krupaya pare pahi murare. From Bhaja Govindam by Adi Shankara: The cycle of births and deaths is endless. Oh Lord, kindly help me cross this unsurpassable ocean of the world.

Questions Of A Professor Of Vedanta Philosophy

Professor:

Babaji, when You came out of Your Tapasya after five years, did You have a vision like Lord Buddha of the cosmic forces and the realities of both animal and human existence?

BABA:

Based on my experience in Tapas, I would like to call the 'cosmic forces' as One Single Self that exists as Supreme Consciousness of the Awareness of Existence. This happens when mind totally stops imagining anything. That is when it loses its ego and the ability to define and it becomes one with the Self's existence. This is the Ultimate Truth. Now the existence of the human and animal bodies: these are the physical matters which come into existence, called birth, and perishes, which is called death. This is not the Self or Ultimate Truth. This is part of the illusory imagination.

Professor:

Did You have some definite conceptions about the Law of Karma, Reincarnatio' and Nirvana?

BABA:

When the body is in action called karma, mind also gets involved into imaginations of actions. That is what binds one into acquiring mental habits of 'I am doing', and 'I am getting'. In fact, reincarnation happens based on the intensity of mind's habits, called thoughts. If, during the action—called karma of the body—the mind, which is consciousness of existence, can keep quiet through practice of austerities, then one can avoid reincarnation and attain Nirvana— when the consciousness of the self, called mind, need not see any birth or scene and can remain in supreme consciousness of existence, the nature of which is Supreme Peace.

Professor:

And what is Your role in this cyclic pattern of human existence: birth, death through suffering, and reincarnation?

BABA:

As all birth, death and suffering happen due to the imagining habits of the conscious energy called mind, our role is to make humanity understand these effects and help them to erase all acquired habits caused by imaginations of the mind—to stop further imaginations, to become one with the Self—what you call nirvana or liberation or enlightenment; just like the sun's ray going back to the sun. We also to help them achieve peace and harmony, as long as the physical body is alive.

Professor:

It is said that we are living in a dark age, that is Kali Yuga. Now, surrounded by consumerism and terrorism, humankind, especially those who live in big cities, have lost peace and tranquility of mind. Are some of the afflicted people, both in India and abroad, coming to you for solace of life and solace of death?

BABA:

As we move and tour different parts of the world and also receive people here in our ashram, we see that many come for peace and solace. In fact, knowingly or unknowingly, everybody is looking for this peace and happiness and liberation from suffering.

Professor:

On the other hand, definitely, You have marked that there are some genuine persons who are looking for a better life style through yoga and meditation.

BABA:

Whereas many look for instant solutions for their unhappiness and sufferings, without trying to go for austerities called sadhana, to control the mind, there are definitely genuine spiritual truth seekers who are looking for a Realized Master and proper guidance in a right direction. Many westerners are quite familiar with our scriptures and are able to appreciate Yogis. They understand and appreciate transparent teachings.

Professor:

To them (westerners), what sort of Yoga do You teach? For instance, Karma Yoga, Jnana Yoga, Bhakti Yoga, Raja Yoga or Sir Aurobindo's Integral Yoga.

BABA:

To all such truth seekers, Baba teaches mainly Dhyana Yoga along with Karma Yoga and Bhakti Yoga. Dhyana Yoga can give both Jnana (knowledge) and Bhakti (devotion).

Professor:

In the west, after two great wars, many young people, now in thousands, have been turning to Indian spirituality since the 1960's. What is their actual quest?

BABA:

Yes, now the youth are turning towards spirituality. For the majority, the quest is for Truth, peace and that which can give peaceful co-existence on this earth.

Professor:

As a result of it, yoga, meditation, guru, all these sacred words have been profaned through advertisement and commercialism. What do You think of the rising evil forces in religion worldwide which have now engulfed Indian spirituality?

BABA:

It is sad that these teachings are made as a market commodity and many Gurus have become like market commodities. A Guru shall appeal to people to learn by truth and without showing unnecessary gimmicks to attract crowds. As far as money is concerned, the ancient practice is that a Guru shall impart the knowledge and wisdom of the Truth to the earnest genuine truth seeker without entering into any type of contract for money. The disciple, on his or her own capacity, shall donate as dakshina, so that the Guru can sustain life and the institution established to impart such knowledge.

Professor:

Under the circumstances, it is very difficult for a genuine seeker after truth, especially who comes from the west, to get the right guru, who is not after money, but after Truth.

BABA:

First it is essential that the seeker is really genuine about what he or she wants and sincere to one's own Self. Then the Divine will definitely show the path. Either the Guru will come to the devotee or the devotee would be guided to such a Guru, who shall impart true knowledge. The inner voice will guide.

Professor:

I think, You are such a Yogi who is after Truth and present the essence of Indian spirituality as a culture—as a discipline of life through which any individual can attain salvation in life. Do You think You can carry on this difficult task by touring abroad, surrounded by fear, anger and hatred, culminating in social violence and terrorism? Or perhaps is it a better idea to train selected westerners in Your ashram and send them to their home towns to organize societies according to Your spiritual disciplines?

BABA:

Whether Baba will go touring or remain in His ashram, the basic mission shall remain the same. Help devotees to learn and get trained, practically. Baba is guided by the Divine Guru. As ordained and with opportunity provided by the Divine Guru, Baba would go on working. Though this is a very hard task, yet we would enjoy putting in efforts and leave the rest to the Divine Guru. Wherever we are, we would try to influence people to build better societies and better world, where humanity can live for each other by practicing mind control, which in turn can give ability in self restraint.

Transcribed From *Shivarudra Balayogi Speaks*, Recorded At The Dehradun Ashram In 2000

Devotee:

What should be our attitude towards thoughts in meditation? How do we deal with them?

BABA:

Mind always does have a tendency to analyze the thoughts and thus recognizes them and in the process gets involved consciously. Analyzing means dualities, just like this is good, this is bad, this is right, this is wrong, why this, why not, and so on. Whereas analyzing and judging are necessary for the universal life, you have to abandon these to go towards enlightenment. That any number of thoughts come is no problem. Just do not recognize, do not analyze, and don't make any judgments as to what they are. Just watch as a witness. Very soon, thoughts will recede and the mind starts getting concentrated to go introvert. Thoughts that arise, first, are not your fault. They are the brain's reflections, so just allow them to happen. The moment you sit for meditation, churning of the mind takes place, and all the subconscious things that are recorded in the mind get evaporated through meditation. These are called: the acquired habits of the mind. During this process, you experience thousands of thoughts arising. So just allow it to happen. Allow the evaporation process to happen and thus the mind gets purified and gets receded towards introvert.

Devotee:

How forcefully does a person concentrate on the bhrikuti, the space in between the eyebrows?

BABA:

For this process, just be polite and firm. Do not try to force. Gradual practice is better. Slowly and slowly you have to practice. What I suggest is, if it becomes difficult to concentrate on the bhrikuti, try to lower the vision, try to see at the tip of the nose. For a few months one can practice like this. Gradually one will be able to lift the eyeballs vision to the level of bhrikuti, or it will happen on its own. Slow and gradual practice done skillfully is better.

Devotee:

Could Baba discuss falling asleep in meditation?

BABA:

Sleep is a state of the brain. It is essential that you do not fall asleep during meditation. Mind is the Self's conscious awareness. If the brain goes to sleep, temporarily the mind loses consciousness of the world, but still it exists. During sleep the brain is active to some extent. When the brain is active in any manner, it catches hold of the uncontrolled mind. This is how you dream during sleep, a short illusion. All this makes you unable to control the mind. So it is essential that you would have taken sufficient rest when you sit for meditation. Also it is essential that after taking food you would have taken rest to allow sufficient time to get the food digested to sit for meditation. The brain should be alert and active. You need this until the mind is able to go beyond intelligence. So you have to keep the brain alert. Even during samadhi also, you experience the awareness of your existence. You are only unconscious of the universe, the world, what is called the drishya, 'the scene' in Sanskrit spiritual terminology. So, during meditation, you must keep yourself conscious and alert. Only gradually you shall lose the consciousness of the universe, your body, your surroundings, and you regain the consciousness of your Real Self that is the Immortal Soul.

Devotee:

Swamiji did not give a mantra at meditation initiation. However, he told me individually that it was okay to use a mantra. Could you please comment about the use of mantra during the practice of Dhyana?

BABA:

It is true, Shri Swamiji did not give a mantra with meditation initiation. I have seen Swamiji saying okay for the mantra, seeing a particular temperament of the devotee, or when a devotee would repeatedly ask whether he or she could repeat a mantra. He would say, "Okay." Shri Swamiji allowed sadhaks, if they were in the habit of repeating mantras or any other type of sadhana, they could do it before or after meditation. Repeating a mantra enables, or assists in mind's concentration and, eventually, you go to meditation. Meditation means: your attention. Your mind's concentration is towards the mantra during its repetition. Without a mantra, gradually your attention gets turned to the Real Self, knowingly or unknowingly. Here knowingly means, you try to concentrate your attention with the imagination of ignorance about the Self, its location or its formation and so on. Unknowingly means, you concentrate your attention on the Self, without any imagination. This is what was taught by Shri Swamiji, enabling the concentration of the mind to go back and settle into the Real Self, ultimately, which is the recommended goal. Thus, as Shri Swamiji taught, in the highest way.

Devotee:

What is the most important thing to remember about the practice of Dhyana?

BABA:

To the practice of Dhyana, you have to dedicate yourself. Be disciplined, have patience and totally surrender. Try to sacrifice the ego. Dedicating means, you have to take out the time in priority and sit down to practice. Be disciplined means, you have to apply discipline to yourself, so that you practice daily, without fail. You become very serious and seriously you pursue. You shall not stop under any circumstances. Then, when you sit down, it takes time for the mind to settle down, because the mind has gone out, consciously, and is always conscious of the universe. It keeps on thinking, and in the process, goes into craving, and constantly picturizes. It cannot keep quiet. So this mind has acquired these habits from time immemorial, perhaps since so many lives. It will take some time, definitely, to control this mind, to purify this mind, so you've got to have patience and allow it to happen.

Surrender: if you do not try to analyze or make any judgments, if you do not jump into any conclusions, do not imagine, then the mind surrenders. The mind, if it surrenders, will recede. It becomes purified. It starts going introvert towards the Self, to the Ultimate Truth, consciously. Sacrificing the ego is also the same. You do not imagine or try to define your existence. You simply experience your existence. You do not try to imagine, do not try to analyze or jump to conclusions, do not try to make any judgments. Don't see any faults in the Guru. Do not try to analyze the Guru. Just have total, unconditional faith in the Guru. That can work wonders, and thus you can sacrifice the ego. Ego is the biggest hurdle to further progress for mankind.

Devotee:

If one does not have a full hour, is it all right to sit for less?

BABA:

My Guru always insisted that we sit at least for one hour. It is necessary for a sadhak because for the first forty minutes, the mind struggles. Only in the end, the last five or ten minutes, one is likely to get some concentration. So it is essential to utilize this five or ten minutes, during which the mind is likely to get concentrated. The first forty minutes will be simply warming up. So if you get up before that, even before you are warmed up and ready to meditate, you are stopping the practice. You are abandoning it. However, in the beginning, it becomes very difficult. It's all right to sit for less, but gradually one must increase to at least one hour for a sadhak. Imagine when we did Tapas. After achieving the concentration of the mind, in between the bhrikuti, when the mind becomes totally purified, it sacrifices all imaginations totally, 100 percent. Only then the real meditation starts. Like that, after it starts, we have to sit for at least seven hours at a stretch, in three shifts. I used to do that way, as instructed and ordained by Swamiji—early morning until mid-noon, after a half hour rest, from mid-noon until night, and in the night, after having a little bit of soup or some vegetables and after a half hour rest, again I used to sit until early morning.

Imagine this was after twenty years of service, after having the physical guidance of Swamiji, who removed my ego, who had adopted so many methods, because I had authorized Swamiji; I had surrendered. After these twenty years of Tapas, in the form of service, for five years we had to do meditation. Only then it became Tapas. If you can concentrate in between eyebrows, on bhrikuti, without any thoughts, simply in a purified state for more than seven to eight hours, that becomes known as Tapas. So now you can understand how necessary it is for a sadhak to sit for at least one hour.

Devotee:

Please discuss the discouragement felt about the lack of progress made in meditation.

BABA:

A sadhak, the one who meditates, should not really bother about progress, should simply surrender to the Guru. Just adopt the methods taught by Guru with full faith. Every time you try to know about progress, your concentration gets distracted. You start trying to analyze, making judgments about your own self and your own progress. Only an expert teacher can know the progress. It's better to think positively always. Reassure yourself that the Guru is with you. He is protecting you. Just concentrate on the practice of meditation. When you worry about progress, your concentration gets distracted. You have to stop, to look back, thus your practice gets distracted; it is stopped. So your attention goes somewhere else and in the process you get involved. You won't be able to progress then. Say you are going in a train from New Delhi to Bangalore. It is a super, fast express but if you want to get down at every station to find out how much you have traveled, how much you have progressed, you are likely to miss the train. You will have to stop there and wait for another train to come. So do not get down off the train. You will have to be sitting in the train. It's like this. So you have to be practicing constantly, simply. Practicing is your duty. Just do not bother about progress. The teacher knows. The teacher is with you. The Guru is with you always. He will help you.

Devotee:

What are some of the signs of successful practice of Dhyana?

BABA:

You become more introvert and peaceful. You are able to appreciate peace and tranquility. In the beginning, after you achieve concentration, after some advancement in meditation, you are likely to experience your blissful nature. This bliss increases and finally goes to the Supreme blissful nature. But you have to wait and carry on. Go beyond this; achieve total peace finally, because peace is the recommended goal. Peace is your abode and you, yourself, are the abode of peace, are the form of peace. You are that total peace and Supreme Peace, consciously existing. One shall experience bliss enormously before achieving peace. Bliss is not the goal. When you are in total blissful nature, you are likely to become excited and in the process the mind jumps back to the world. It's likely to experience the 'jumping', and it will come back to the existence. So it is essential you hold on to the sadhana even if you are experiencing bliss. During bliss, you are likely to experience trembling, excitement. You might feel like dancing. You might feel like opening your eyes and laughing and so many things. You might feel like going into trance, also. But this is not the recommended goal. You have to wait. You have to become peaceful, serene, composed, introvert. Peace is the recommended goal. Your mind's imagination has to decrease, decrease, and totally vanish. Thereby, it has to surrender to the Divine Guru. Actual surrender takes place only when your imagination stops, when the mind recedes. Thus the mind learns to remain in God-Consciousness and becomes single-pointed. It settles down to the Self peacefully.

Devotee:

Are there any mistakes that can be made in the practice of Dhyana?

BABA:

Instead of practicing the concentration with attention, you are likely to grip on the mind and allow the mental consciousness to run after thoughts, thereby increasing the mental imaginations to many fold and magnified. Ego is another problem, which will always make you commit mistakes, particularly during sadhana. You are likely to lose concentration. Very often you are likely to become careless, by trying to postpone the practice. That is why, previously, I had emphasized on discipline and dedication. Forgetting the Guru's instructions during initiation, and doing something else is also very likely. Losing faith is another problem. So you should never lose faith. Faith in the name of the Guru can work wonders. It will always inspire you. You require inspiration. You have to draw inspiration from the Guru. You have to pray constantly, so that you shall not commit any mistakes.

Mind always has a tendency to analyze and judge, as I have already told you. In the process, it gets involved consciously (with thoughts) and keeps on running. That's a mistake in meditation. Your job is to practice and allow the mind to get absorbed into the Self. Your job is just concentrate without trying to imagine anything. When you do not imagine anything and just concentrate, you pay your attention to the Real Self only.

The brain is in touch with the universe through the nervous system and other sensory organs. So in the process, when it receives and it orders, the brain reflects in a de-codified message. Just like, if you are hungry you get a sensation in the stomach that is transmitted to the brain. The brain tells you that you are hungry and the mind, the consciousness, catches it and experiences that you are hungry, because consciously you get involved. Just like you are watching a movie. Though technically, biologically, in any way, you are not at all involved with that movie, as you go on watching, unknowingly, consciously you get involved and you start imagining your own self into that movie. You experience the happiness and sorrows of the movie as your own, because your consciousness has got involved. It has been sucked into that movie. The same way the soul's consciousness gets involved into the reflections of the brain and in the process takes the shape of the brain's reflections and it runs and it runs.

So thus, that is why you have been advised not to try to analyze and make any judgments (during meditation). Just keep watching as a witness. Thus you can avoid mistakes. If you are unable to dedicate, be disciplined and have patience, if you are unable to sacrifice your ego and surrender to the Guru, if you are unable to have faith in the Guru, you will always be committing a mistake. Just be careful.

Devotee:

After meditating for many years, I began to experience the feeling that who I had felt myself to be, had dissolved. I could no longer identify myself in a specific way. I felt a kind of expansiveness but it was very uncomfortable. I felt myself to be a vast emptiness with no sense of meaning or purpose. At times, I would alternate between feeling very expanded and blissful and then would come contractions of awareness that were very painful. There was a lot of pain and fear during this period. At times I became very discouraged. Could you please comment on this state, give some encouragement regarding these difficulties?

BABA:

A very important question. Pay your attention. When you say that you began to experience 'feeling', who is this who feels? As long as there are feelings, there are thoughts. Thoughts are imaginations and it is the mind that imagines. Here the mind has tried to imagine the Self. You have to experience the Self, not imagine the Self. I repeat, you have got to experience the Self and not imagine. Because of the imagination, there were further feelings of expansiveness and emptiness. Gradually it can give rise to fear. Thoughts occur to the mind in this process. The mind has got confused. Do not get discouraged. Mind need not get confused.

The existence of the Self is of supreme consciousness. When you experience this, you become aware of your real existence. Then you lose all imaginations and definitions. You are simply aware of your existence. That is the Supreme Peace, beyond even supreme bliss. You don't feel any definitions about your existence. You don't have any feelings of the body, of the surroundings. When there are no feelings, an awareness of the Self can occur. You will always be able to remain in that consciousness, which is only Supreme Peace, serene peace. Don't worry, wait for that. That's why I told you that you require patience. You have to wait. Allow it to happen. Whatever experience you get other than the peace is the mind's imagination, illusion. That's why it is called illusion, because the mind imagines and hypnotizes itself. The meditation helps you to liberate yourself from this hypnotizing effect.

This becomes possible when you are able to do Tapas, when you are able to concentrate without any thoughts for at least seven to eight hours at a stretch. That is Tapas. The Self does not require anything for its existence. The Self is Supreme Peace. Do not feel disheartened. You are going on the right path. Until the mind is able to remain peaceful, effortlessly, have faith and reassure yourself. The Guru is with you and he will protect you always. Go ahead. Do not stop the practice. Just wait and watch as a witness.

Devotee:

In the west there are proponents of Advaita and especially the teachings of Ramana Maharshi who place little emphasis on meditation. They encourage knowing the Self in the present and discourage reliance on any progressive techniques, like meditation.

BABA:

I honor Ramana Maharshi and offer my salutations to Him, but if people place little emphasis on the teaching of meditation and encourage only the Self-Inquiry, and if they discourage meditation, by condemning it, they are committing a mistake. They are 'half-baked beans'. They are not the perfect ones. They have also not understood Self-Inquiry. In fact, what Ramana Maharshi taught, what Shri Shivabalayogi taught are all the same. If you have to enquire about the Self, there must be some technology. If you simply try to think and go on thinking, "Who am I? Who am I? Who am I?" thoughts will arise, imaginations will arise and, in the process, you again hypnotize yourself, as to who you really are. But actually what Ramana Maharshi tried to tell was, "Observe from where the existence of the Self's consciousness is arising." This observance is nothing but meditation. Observing the Self's existence, consciousness arising means you have to pay attention to the arising of the Self's consciousness. Paying attention means, you meditate. That is Dhyana. Dhyana means: your attention to.

Thus, meditation and observing the Self, 'Who am I?' are all the same. You have to apply a method that is technology, the techniques. Thus, my Guru, Swamiji, also taught the highest way of realizing the Self. Just like Ramakrishna Paramahamsa also said, "A salt doll, trying to know the depth of the sea, jumped in, and in the process became one with It." When you observe from where the consciousness of the Self is arising, your mind gets absorbed into It. Meditation is also the same. That's why Swamiji also initiated by telling, "Do not imagine anything. Just pay your attention. Concentrate your mind and sight." So when the mind gets concentrated, gradually, because it stops thinking, then you are able to meditate. When it stops thinking, it gets purified, loses its imagination. So, its attention towards the world decreases and it goes introvert. When it goes introvert, it gains the ability to observe the inner, Real Self. That is the real meditation. So when it observes, meditates like this, this mind gradually gets absorbed into the Self, and you get enlightenment. You become one with the Self. That is the recommended goal. Thus, meditation (Dhyana) is the same (as Self-Inquiry). It is the highest technique, the highest way. Through meditation also, you will know the Self in the present, because you will lose the past and the future. If you have imaginations of the mind, you're always brooding about the past or you are anxious about the future. But when you meditate, you lose both these affects of the mind, and it gets neutralized, comes to the present. It gets absorbed into the Self. Thus, you will become simply being. You exist; this is what you achieve through meditation also. It's only the difference in terminology. Actually there is no difference in meditation and Ramana Maharshi's teachings. It is all the same.

Devotee:

Could you comment on the role of personal effort and the role of Guru's Grace in spiritual growth?

BABA:

The Guru's grace is always flowing like the river. You have to put in personal effort, with all your faith and surrender to catch the Guru's Grace. That is essential. Faith and your efforts should go together. The Guru's Grace is always there.

Devotee:

Could you comment on the relationship in between Satguru or inner Guru and the outer Guru, manifested in human form?

BABA:

The inner Guru and the outer Guru are really one and the same, provided the outer Guru is a Jivanmukta, a Realized and Enlightened Soul. Then the disciple will be very lucky, the luckiest one. If the outer Guru is a Yogi, then the inner Guru and outer Guru are both the same.

Devotee:

How does the manifested Guru help the devotee receive Divine Grace in our lives, which we feel to be associated with a real person, helping to make real things happen? How does that work?

BABA:

Actually, your mind is connected to the Divine, just like the sun's rays come out of the sun and are part of the sun only. In the same way, the mind has come out of the actual Divine, so it is part of the

Divine. But, because the mind's consciousness is in the universe, it is unable to touch the Divine. That's why prayers are taught and also meditation is taught. If you pray, your mind gets concentrated. If you can pray with all your concentration, your mind can go introvert. When it touches the Divine—the mind's original source—then the Divine's Grace starts flowing automatically. It is called Automatic Divine Activity. If your previous or past mental resolutions, called sankalpas, were very, very strong and devotional, gradually with devotional practice and surrender to the Guru, that concentration becomes stronger and stronger. Then it goes introvert and it touches the Divine. Then the Guru manifests, when the time is ripe.

When the ego has been sacrificed and the mind has receded considerably, then the prayers do touch the Divine. Then that Divine, the real Guru manifests in that form on which your mind had already resolved. For a long time like that, become devoted and surrendered with all faith. So the Divine manifests in that form and will help the devotee. This is how the things work. That is why you must constantly pray and meditate. In due course of time, the inner Guru can manifest and help, if you have a mission. Otherwise also, the Divine will always help. The Divine will manifest physically, if you have a mission. The Divine has to guide in that form, if your mental resolutions are like that.

My mental resolutions were always on Swamiji, Shri Shivabalayogi, as I have told you earlier. I met Swamiji in February 1971. The first moment I saw Him, I fell in love with Him. My mind was instantly and totally drawn to Him. Until this day, it is unwavering, even when Swamiji Himself wanted to test this devotion, when Swamiji was physically with us. This faith was unwavering. I could see and monitor this. If the faith becomes unwavering, then the Divine has to appear one day. Constantly I used to pray also, with total concentration, until the time was ripe and the detachment was total. I think this certainly takes time. You have to keep on doing sadhana; put in your efforts and pray for the grace of the Divine. When the time is ripe, one day that does happen. It's an Automatic Divine Activity.

Devotee:

Could Baba please explain the mechanics of the phenomenon of world appearance arising from imagination? How is it that meditation takes us out of the grip of this illusion?

BABA:

This is a very difficult question to answer to a sadhak at initial stages, because even if I explain completely a sadhak will not be able to understand properly. This is explained by the Guru, taught by the inner Guru, just before samadhi or during samadhi, only when the understanding capability has increased to the maximum. However, I will try to give you some clues about this.

Just watch your mind. Everything will appear to you as your mind imagines and recognizes and identifies. So, gradually like this, a world, a universe, has sat in your mind. So, your mind is always conscious of the world, the universe. It is thinking, it is analyzing, it is concluding. It always picturizes, imagines and magnifies things to its capacity, to its will. As it runs, the world shall appear to you according to your own imagination. It is the mind that experiences. Also, if you start imagining about one particular thing, its picture starts coming to you. The mind imagines, and if your mind continues in the same imagination, with total concentration—the more the mind becomes concentrated—the imagined figure, the picture in your mind, becomes more and more strong and solid. So thus, if your mind's imagination with concentration can be increased to its highest pitch, the vision, the imagination becomes the mental projection in the next state. Ultimately, if it can reach the stage of Tapas, that is when you obtain the maximum concentration and the mind is unaware of anything else, except that particular one imagination. Then the manifestation takes place.

This small mind which we call 'our' mind—we human beings say, "It's my mind. It's your mind." This has come out of a small imagined self called the jivatman. This mind can work such wonders. People have become genius through this mental concentration and application on the brain. They have been able to use the brain to the maximum. So these people are called genius in the universe. If this small mind with its concentration can work wonders, imagine the All-Pervading Spirit, the Divine's mental strength. If something happens due to the Divine, how powerful it becomes. Thus, the manifestation of the world happens. Even science believes in the Big Bang. Spirituality also says that when the consciousness raises to the level of the universe, to the imagination of the Universe, (there is) violence. To recede this violence, we use meditation.

Some people have asked me the question, "Is meditation hypnotizing one's own self?" No, not at all. Actually, imagination is hypnotizing. You have imagined. You imagine something and your mental consciousness gets into the grip of this illusion called imagination, thus hypnotizing one's own self to that particular imagination-illusion. Meditation is the reverse journey, the liberation from this hypnotizing, the liberation from this imagination-illusion. In meditation the initiation is given and you are being asked not to imagine anything, not to repeat anything, just keep watching. So when you are able to do this, concentration occurs and gradually the mind loses its imagination. Thus, it gets liberated from the illusion of definitions that it had given to so many things. To so many things it had recognized, it had imagined. So thus, you get liberated from all illusions and your mental consciousness settles back to the Self's existence. You become aware of your Self.

Devotee:

I have felt a lot of bliss and a strong sense of being guided always by the Divine Presence. Sometimes the individual seems to be there, but the strong attachment to the fulfillment of personal desire is much less. There is much deeper satisfaction in sensing the blissfulness of Divine Grace and will operating. Could Baba please discuss this stage and how to go beyond—to experience our own pure existence, beyond the bliss.

BABA:

This is good, quite an advanced stage. But you will have to be equally very, very careful. As I have already told you, the blissfulness stage is quite risky also. The mind will try to jump back to the universe by giving you lots of such experiences, out of imagination and illusions. It will try to define and in the process get sucked back; the mind will come into existence. So, you will have to ignore every experience at this stage and just try to concentrate on the consciousness of your own existence. Try that. You will definitely find the inner Guru will inspire you. You will have to have patience. The desire itself has to recede and gradually vanish. You have to wait for this to happen. It will happen. Do not try to define, even as Divine's Grace. Don't try to give any definitions, whether it's blissfulness or what it is. Just stop this also and do not allow the mind to think or define.

Stop the desire to achieve peace also. Then you will achieve peace. It is just like this: you're always thinking and repeating, "I want to go to deep sleep. I want to go to deep sleep. I want to go to deep sleep." But because the mind is always thinking, it doesn't recede; it doesn't allow the brain to rest, so you don't go into sleep. So when the deep sleep occurs, it suddenly occurs, and you don't know. In the same way, the desire to achieve samadhi, the experience of pure existence, should also recede. Finally then, you will be led, you will go to that pure existence of your consciousness. Don't worry. You will definitely be a blessed one and it will happen soon. You just be have patience and continue to pay attention on the existence without trying to analyze, without trying to make any judgments. Do not define anything. Don't even think of the name of the Divine at this stage also. Just keep quiet.

Devotee:

Baba has said that during Tapas, Swamiji gave techniques for the complete eradication of the ego. Could you please discuss these techniques with us?

BABA:

First thing, you will have to have faith and surrender. Surrender means, do not try to mentally imagine anything that happens. Just keep watching as a witness. Don't relate yourself to that experience.

It's only a thing that you will have to watch, so that it gets evaporated and the mind recedes. Even the imagination of the existence of the Self is also recognized as ego in spiritual terms. This is the final ego, which will vanish just before samadhi. This will happen. But you have to surrender mentally. This means, you do not think anything. You don't bother, even if thoughts occur, even if any visions occur. If any experiences occur, do not try to define what it is. Mentally you have to lose all imaginations. If the time is ripe, the mind itself will understand. The mind has to understand that it is imagining. The mind has to stop.

When you go deeper and deeper, the inner Guru will definitely help you. Until then, you try to surrender. Whenever a small thought occurs, just try to stop it. Do not give attention to the thought and your mind will stop. Because, the moment a thought occurs, the mind tries to analyze it, watches and gets involved into that thought; it recognizes the thought. It tries to define the thought. So do not recognize the thought. Do not recognize any experience that occurs, even if it's blissfulness, it's Divine's Grace, or anything—no definition, nothing! And pray to Swamiji; pray to the inner Guru to bless you, for this to happen.

Devotee:

Could Baba please discuss bhava samadhi and it's relationship to Dhyana?

BABA:

Bhava samadhi literally means feelings. The mind is constantly wavering, constantly is taking these different shapes. These are called thoughts. The thoughts are the technical basis for feelings. The thoughts give rise to feelings. When a thought occurs, you try to feel it. The mind itself takes the shape and goes into a feeling. Samadhi is stillness, stand stillness. Well, Swamiji saw devotees could not go into meditation, directly. They used to argue that they can do anything they want out of their own will. Then Swamiji wanted to teach them that there is a greater Divine power that's working, and everybody is guided and inspired by the Divine power. So he blessed some devotees to go into bhava. Bhava samadhi is blessed to a devotee to give him some experience of the single-pointedness of the mind, so that eventually he can achieve some concentration; he will learn to pay attention and go into deeper meditation. Swamiji once gave me a definition in His own way, saying that when a person goes into bhava samadhi, that particular person has the vision of his Ishtadeva—the Divine, the Deity that is dearer to him or her. Others may seek some action in thier body. This bhava samadhi should enable one to achieve some concentration, single-pointedness of the mind. So one gets a vision of a Deity and the mind is absorbed to that Deity, that particular vision. You keep watching and thus, you go into a blissful state. This blissful state, depending on one's nature, might make the body move in excitement, sometimes. Thus, others may see some action in that body.

But this is like giving some lollipop to a child, to make it go to the school. But, unfortunately, people sometimes get stuck to the lollipop and they don't go to the school. Going to the school means, eventually you have to go to meditation again, to achieve Self-Realization, the recommended goal. Thus this bhava samadhi, if this experience is understood properly, this can always help in meditation, to achieve some concentration in the beginning. You are able to pay attention to the Real Self, to meditate.

Real bhava samadhi also is a culmination of long time devotional practices, which will give you faith and devotion. That's why Bhakti Marga (the devotional path) is taught. It's your consciousness towards the Deity, your attention to the Deity, which gradually shall give single-pointedness to your mind. But this is also not very easy. This is the genuine bhava samadhi, which will enable you to go introvert, deeper into meditation eventually. But you have to be really devoted to the Deity, not try to claim yourself as if being possessed by some Divine. The more a person experiences real bhava samadhi, the more one will go introvert. The more one will go introvert, less and less they have to claim. This means they don't have anything to claim. They stop claiming anything. They become quiet and go introvert and then they can go into meditation properly, not otherwise.

Everything else is simply a waste of energy and time. Hardly anybody will achieve by talking through bhava samadhi, by giving instructions. In spirituality, any of your efforts, the sadhana, should enable your mind to recede. Ego receding means: eradication of the ego, the mind recedes. If the mind is in existence, it will always imagine. Because, the mind will be in existence only when it imagines. Thus every imagination is bondage. So you can understand, if your efforts can enable your mind to recede, only then you are able to achieve something. But if it becomes more excited or more violent, the mind will be in existence and you will be hypnotizing yourself more and more with imaginations and illusions. So you must be careful. Every individual must be careful if they are genuinely interested to go towards Enlightenment. They should not imagine and deceive themselves by claiming to be some divine authority. One has to very careful about bhava samadhi.

Devotee:

At the completion of Shri Shivabalayogi's Tapas and at the completion of Baba's Tapas, there was a manifestation of Shiva-Parvati (Ardharishwara). Was this a physical manifestation for the purpose of Darshan? Do God and Guru actually manifest in physical form that you can see and touch?

BABA:

Yes, the manifestation was in physical form. It was for the purpose of Darshan and for eradication of the final resolution— to guide you to go beyond samadhi towards the effortless Nirvikalpa Samadhi. They do actually manifest, both the God and Guru, in a physical form that you can see and touch. As I was telling you earlier, look at the imagination of your mind. You imagine and concentrate. If both the things can happen together, this means your imagination will sit on one particular thing. This is the beginning of devotion. That is how it is taught. So thus, your concentration sits on one Deity. Just like, when I saw Swamiji in 1971, I was completely thoroughly and totally drawn to Swamiji. So that was the resolution set in the mind. Well, eventually Swamiji trained me to remove that resolution also, just before Nirvikalpa Samadhi so that I lost that resolution. But because of that strong resolution previously, the Divine had to come as Shiva and Parvati, the Divine had to come as Shivabalayogi. Then the mind realized that was also an illusion, a mental manifestation, finally. Not the mental manifestation of my imagined self, it was the mental manifestation of the All-Pervading, the Boundless Divine. Then you go to Nirvikalpa Samadhi, where only one single Self exists.

I would like to say this occurs in three stages. First, the mind's imagination state. It starts imagining. As the imagination and concentration on that imagination become stronger and stronger, the vision also becomes more and more stronger and solid. Gradually you lose the sense that you're trying to imagine. When it grows devotionally, you start losing your imagination of your own existence. Your concentration simply grows on the Deity that you love. To your consciousness, only that Deity exists. Then the second stage, mental projection happens. That's when the great devotees have always felt the presence of the Divine, the Divine Guru or their Lord, their Deity. Thus, one always has the experience, blissful experience. That is not a feeling. That is a little higher stage. This is also not easy. This can happen only in an advanced state of sadhana, whether in the Bhakti Marga, or in meditation. It will happen. The projection takes place. Later on, in the third stage, when your concentration rises to the highest pitch, what is called Tapas, this Tapas enables to evaporate your imagined self, totally. Only the Deity exists. So that is when the mind recedes totally and merges into the Divine. But it's not actually Nirvikalpa Samadhi. When it merges, it has merged with the resolution. So an iota of resolution still remains. Then the manifestation of the Divine occurs. Whatever the previous resolutions you have, that will happen in the physical form. That is the technology of the Divine. The Divine has such a power. But if you can pray, if your mind can touch the Divine with 100 percent concentration, with a particular resolution, then the manifestation happens. But this is a very rare phenomenon, very, very difficult one. It's not as easy as I am talking. It has to happen naturally and effortlessly. It happened to us, maybe because of previous practices, from time immemorial, through so many lives. Such a concentration came when I first saw Swamiji and that resolution stood in the mind. So, before entering into the Nirvikalpa of the Pure Existence, this experience of the manifestation was given and then the Nirvikalpa Samadhi occurs and everything is gone. Only a single Self simply exists with peace and peace and peace.

Devotee:

When we feel discouraged, or that faith in God and Guru are challenged, what would Baba suggest?

BABA:

Satsang—the company of good people, the knowers of the truth of spirituality—is suggested so that your discouragement gets converted into positive courage, through constant company, in some manner. Either through physical presence, if it's possible, or through some other means of communication. In modern times, you have telephone, e-mail, letters and so many other things. Thus you can constantly keep in touch with such people who are Enlightened. If that is possible, that's wonderful. If you can be in touch with such people who are really Enlightened, and try to share your experiences—discouragement, depression, or anything sincerely, and get guidance and their company. If the faith in God and Guru are challenged, you must go to the company of such great people, so that they will guide you always. They will inspire you not to get discouraged and to have constant faith, without any reservations to the God and Guru.

Never allow any challenge to go un-faced. Face such a challenge. Reassure yourself again and again, repeatedly and repeatedly, that the Divine and Guru are in your heart; that Guru is yours, your own Father and Mother who will protect you. Whatever work the Guru is doing, it might appear to you happy or unhappy. Just do not try to judge. Allow it to happen. Reassure yourself, even if it is unhappiness or upheavals in the life. Just reassure yourself, that the Guru is working to remove the destiny of prarabdha karma, the previous resolutions of the mind, which have caused the mind to go into egotism. The Guru is working even if you are being tortured sometimes. Even if you have to experience the bitterness of life. Because, the operation may always be bitter. That's why you have to authorize your Guru, just like if a doctor has to operate upon your body, you have to sign the papers and authorize the doctor. Thus you have to authorize the Guru, so that the Guru can operate on you strongly, even if it is bitter. The company of the good people, the knowers of the truth, Ultimate Truth, those who are enlightened, is always the recommended suggestion.

Questions Asked To Baba By E-mail Or At Public Programs

Devotee:

Is peace on earth a possibility or is there something in the human condition, such that it cannot happen?

BABA:

Yes, it is definitely possible, if all the people sincerely work towards it. But if you want peace, you have to practice peace.

Devotee: (a little girl)

What does God look like? Is God a girl or a boy?

BABA:

God can look as whatever you wish. If you pray sincerely, God will manifest and bless you directly. You have to love God, then God will appear in whatever form you like. God can become either (a girl or a boy), whichever you want.

Devotee:

Could Baba please talk about the inner Guru and the outer Guru and the relationship between these two?

BABA:

When we talk about the outer Guru, we mean anything in the world, outside ourselves, from which we learn. You may find that

Guru takes a physical form and you get attached to that. Such a thing is only possible by God's grace. When we talk about the inner Guru, we mean God teaching directly, from inside. The outer Guru helps to lead the mind, to becoming concentrated. Then the inner Guru takes over and leads the mind inwards, until it settles down in the Self. The outer Guru will guide you to the inner Guru who will take over the task of teaching.

Devotee:

How is it possible to overcome laziness?

BABA:

First, we need to understand the need to do anything, say to meditate. Just as you understand the need to eat, similarly the meditation is food for the mind. So, you need this understanding, then you'll start automatically.

Devotee:

If a life is taken abruptly, if someone dies abruptly, is it part of God's plan, or is it an accident?

BABA:

There can be no conclusive answer to this. Sometimes it can be an accident. It is important how the mind is in the period before the passing on. That dictates the soul's next birth. If the mind is very fearful, then it can lead to more difficult circumstances in the next birth. But if the mind is brave, calm, non-violent, then the life can elevate in the next birth.

Devotee:

In Baba's Tapas, did He remember his past lives, and if so, did it help your understanding?

BABA:

I simply concentrated on God. All these other things can be distractions from the real target. They are ultimately illusions of the mind. So I didn't concentrate on these things, or it would divert the

attention. I simply concentrated on the Self. It is something like if
you are traveling from here to Sydney on the train, and you keep
getting down at various places to see this and that. If you do that,
you will end up missing the train! You won't reach Sydney. In the
same way, these things are all distractions.

Devotee:

Baba has shown the Brahmari Pranayam breathing exercise. How
does it help?

BABA:

The breathing exercises can 'warm up' the mind to get it ready
for meditation. If the mind is restless, and then you breathe deeply,
you will find the mind starts to rest, to settle. Also, these exercises
take out stress and congestion in the head. The stretches we do after
meditation are because the body may have gone a little stiff during
the meditation, and you need to stretch it gently to avoid hurting
yourself. In the same way, we open the eyes slowly, and then stretch,
so you won't hurt yourself.

Devotee:

I am curious about what you said in a previous answer about the
state of the mind at the time of death dictating the circumstances of
the next birth. Does that mean that all that you've done throughout
the life is not important, and only those thoughts at the end are
important?

BABA:

No, it is not that simple. The mind absorbs all of the imprints
throughout the life. These then play again in the mind subsequently.
There is an old story about this. There was a man who was a great
miser. He was very miserly with his money all the time. He knew he
was going to die eventually, so he decided he would name all of his
sons after the various gods. So he named one son as Krishna, another
as Shiva, and so on. He planned that when he was on his deathbed
he would call out for his sons to come, and so that way he would be
reciting God's name. So when he was on his deathbed, he went on

calling out, "Rama, Krishna, Shiva."and the sons came running to him but he wouldn't die. Then he suddenly remembered something and called out, "Hey, that other fellow owes me money. Make sure you get it from him!" Then he died as he was saying that. So all the plotting and planning was to no avail. He was simply going on thinking about money on his deathbed, just as he had always done throughout his lifetime. This story is to illustrate that the mind's true tendencies will always come out.

Devotee:

I have read in some texts and scriptures how in the Self-Realization process, the kundalini at the base of the spine travels up through the chakra petals to the top of the head. Can You please talk about this?

BABA:

First, one needs to understand that the kundalini is just another portion of the mind, of our consciousness. It is from this portion of the mind that we get bodily awareness. In Tapas, when the mind becomes concentrated, it lifts the kundalini to the top of the head. But this is only for a moment—for the merest fraction—and then the mind and kundalini join and go towards the Self.

Kundalini is the conscious energy of the soul, as the mind is. Both mind and kundalini are the same substances—pure consciousness. One portion is always conscious of the universe; this is known as mind. In other words, mind is a bundle of thoughts. The other part, which has gone into the body, gives you, body consciousness as yourself. After constant sadhana and the descent of divine grace, when the mind becomes single-pointed and concentrated, the kundalini also gets lifted upwards and finally mind and kundalini become One Pure Consciousness and go towards samadhi.

Devotee:

I have been doing a form of breathing meditation occasionally over a period of time, wherein I have developed quite a strong

rotational, vibrational energy in my body. This energy begins when I
practice circular breathing and starts with a vibrational quality. Then
my hands tend to go into tetany, much like the mudras I have heard
about in various practices in India. Then, I seem to be able to get
this energy moving about my body. If really activated, it courses in
the fashion of a bowl. This is in many ways an ecstatic experience,
and I worry that I may become addicted to achieving this state just
for the physical experience, without understanding how it can be
useful.

BABA:

It appears that this has given you bliss. However, you should not
apply this healing energy on anybody because you are likely to loose
it soon after, giving rise to mental agony and different emotions like
lust, anger, frustration, etc. Let me enlighten you a little about mind
and kundalini and their inter-relationship. Actually both mind and
kundalini are the two branches of the same tree called Self, the
Ultimate Truth. With its imaginations and thoughts, in thousands of
ways, a part of your Real Self-Consciousness, has gone into the
universe and you call this as mind. A little bit of this same conscious
energy has gone inside the body and this is called the kundalini, the
coiled energy. Compared to the kundalini, the mind is more powerful
and is widely spread in the universe, consciously with imaginations.
Through meditation, when the mind becomes totally concentrated,
losing all its imaginations in every way, it lifts the kundalini, before
getting de-linked from the intelligence, and starts going towards
samadhi. At this stage, using its emotional energies, the mind tries
to create enormous bliss, which can give rise to excitement. The
mind tries to do this so that it can jump back into imaginations and
run towards the illusion called the universe.

What I feel is, with your breathing meditations, the mind getting
concentrated has been trying to lift the kundalini, and also is creating
ecstasy. Suggestions are that, at this stage you need to have enormous
patience and constantly pray to the Divine Guru to help you to remain
calm. Keep the body also calm and do not allow it to get trapped in
to the enormous vibrational energy that is being produced. Total

mental composure is the remedy to control the body's vibrational movements, including the physical mudras. At that time, remain calm; keep praying. If possible, try to sit in what is called Vajrasana, folding your legs in such a way that the heels are pressing against the hips and your back and neck are strait. This will give you the necessary nervous strength and mental composure, so that you can have normal breathing. Then, with prayers to guide you through to total Self-Realization, may the Divine Guru give you the strength to remain calm. Enormous detachment is also necessary. Suggestions are that, at this stage, do not bother about any mission or helping others. This can happen later when the Divine will ordain. Then try to meditate, focusing the eyes in between eyebrows and remain like a witness. Do not try to analyze about any thoughts or visions. You will progress. It can become dangerous if you try and start using this (energy) just now. Instead this can take you towards Self-Realization, which is the recommended goal, that Supreme Peace.

Devotee:

What is the difference between two people on a sincere spiritual path, when one happens to have an awakened kundalini and the other doesn't?

BABA:

The difference would depend on how much the mind can surrender. In other words, how much can the mind loose imaginations and become quiet? That means the mind is automatically more towards the Divine and becomes eligible to receive Divine blessings automatically—or you can say, automatically Divine grace and blessings start flowing. So, if the mind were more concentrated and single-pointed towards the Divine, automatically kundalini would have awakened. Always both happen together and just one of them does not happen. Actually, awakening of kundalini is the culmination of Yoga, whether Bhakti, Karma, or Dhyana Yoga. It all depends on the mind. That is why the sadhak is taught first to try and control the mind through Bhakti, Karma, or Dhyana Yoga.

The rising of kundalini is always an advantage in progress towards the Divine. There can be other experiences also, both negative and positive. The negative, like burning sensations, confusion, etc., and the positive advantage like if you resolve anything in the mind, it may start happening. But one needs to ignore both positive and negative and quietly praying for the Divine Guru's refuge, protection and inner guidance, should proceed. If enormous bliss is experienced, one is on the right path but should not stop there. Proceed on the path of sadhana until total peace is achieved.

Devotee:

Can You please speak about the chakra energy systems?

BABA:

This chakra system is a terminology used in ancient times to discuss the rise of the kundalini energy. I'll try to explain. The kundalini is nothing but a part of the soul's conscious energy which has gone out into the body, in the same way as the mind has gone out into the world. This gives us the body consciousness. Sadhana is taught to control the mind, because the kundalini is less powerful than the mind. So, if the mind is controlled first, then it draws up the kundalini, and as the kundalini rises, it passes through various chakras, each with its own name: Muladhara, and so on. At the Sahasrara chakra, situated at the top of the head, the mind and kundalini become one. The mind is then de-linked from the brain. This happens just before samadhi. But the sadhak should not worry too much about these things, as all these things distract the mind and can simply build up more new imaginations in the mind. If you bring the mind back to its source, this will all happen by itself.

Devotee:

How important is humility to a sadhak?

BABA:

Humility is very essential. It keeps ego out. If ego is strong, the sadhaks tend to be in a rush, so they can't learn properly. Humility is very necessary, so the sadhak can surrender and develop faith and devotion. If the ego is strong, the student tends to think that after they have heard something once or twice, that they know it fully. "Oh, I have heard Baba say this all before, and I have heard this already. I already understand this." The Guru has to repeat some things very often so that they will penetrate very deeply into the mind, and they need to be repeated until all imaginations of ego and mind are gone.

Devotee:

There are many different ways of meditating: watching the breath, observing a candle flame or flowing water, etc. If they all result in bringing the mind to rest, how is Dhyana better?

BABA:

We honor all meditation techniques. However, in such other meditation techniques, if the mind is watching a particular object or thing, then in the end it will have to abandon that thing or object before it can then go introverted. In Dhyana there is the benefit that no such object will need to be abandoned, as no object is focused on. So, on its own, the mind will go introverted.

Devotee:

What happens to the soul when the body dies?

BABA:

The soul doesn't go anywhere. It doesn't travel. It is all pervasive. Soul is intact, and doesn't change. But the mind will see the next drishya, as we call 'the scene' in spiritual language. When the mind leaves the body, when it is withdrawn from the brain, there is temporary unconsciousness before the next scene.

Devotee:

You said you have seen God. Is that correct?

BABA:

Yes, like I am seeing you now. The manifestation is as solid as I am seeing you now. In the same way I saw Him manifest in front of me. But that is not the end, not the recommended goal. Depending on the mind's previous resolutions, these things may happen. But you have to go beyond that, beyond the mind's thoughts and resolutions, to the thoughtless state.

Devotee:

Why is there evil in the world?

BABA:

God is above and beyond all dualities. If there is suffering in this world, it is because we have failed to look after each other properly. We talk about peace, but we fail to practice peace. We have to look after each other; then all will be happy.

Devotee:

What is intuition? Should we follow that intuition or follow logic?

BABA:

There is no concrete explanation for intuition. Someone feels that an event might happen, and then it happens. It could be just coincidence. Spirituality teaches you to face the moment, not become anxious about the future. There is a natural human tendency to want to know the future. It is better to make efforts in the present to help you face things in the present.

Devotee:

To study we need to focus. That focus is teaching us to be more spiritual. Is that true?

BABA:

Yes. If you are devoted to studying something, then the mind gets concentrated on that. Focus always gives best results in all endeavors. The mind tends to get distracted easily. Meditation helps to focus the mind. If the mind's imaginations are not controlled, then the mind tends to make you dance to its tunes. If you have some money, but it is all scattered on the ground, spread here and there, then it is very difficult to collect them together. But if you have 1,000 dollars all sitting in one single place and if one dollar is scattered, it is easy to collect back that one dollar and make it complete. So all these things such as singing and so on, they all help to give the mind a single-pointedness and are helpful.

Devotee:

Clairvoyance, in which one can see the past, or past life, or even the future, is that natural when one is enlightened?

BABA:

No. When one is enlightened, one sees God everywhere. One doesn't see the individual anymore. So then we pray only to God to help everyone. If one starts looking at the past, present, future, this requires the mind and then you can't help people as effectively because conscious attention is not on God.

Devotee:

If God is good, why is the earth and all the people on the earth allowed to suffer so much?

BABA:

I also felt like this, so I understand your question. But when one becomes enlightened, one finds that God doesn't have any resolutions of the mind. Just like the sun doesn't choose who gets the light, whoever comes in front of the sun gets light. So similarly God is impartial. He doesn't think, "Let these people be happy, but these other people should be unhappy." No, it is not like that. What is needed is that we become nobler. It is our job. God is above all these things. You need to find who you really are; who is really suffering; who is really responsible. God is not involved.

This creation happened due to God, but not according to His wishes. He is not involved in this creation. This is difficult to understand because the mind is use to judging. These problems all occur because the mind is out of control. I suggest you first work out, "Has God created this world?" Instead of getting angry with God for creating, firstly, what evidence do you have that God in fact created this universe? There is a Truth behind this.

Devotee:

Baba said that during Tapas, He lost all individual Atman and became one with the Divine. If Baba lost individuality, how does He still make individual decisions?

BABA:

There are no individual decisions. I go by the guidance of my Father. It is inspiration and the Divine's planning. If anyone invites me to go somewhere, I go there. Thirty years ago Swamiji invited me to Dehradun and I went. The Australian devotees came to Dehradun and invited me to Perth, so I came. Everything is designed by my Guru. None of it is my own resolutions.

Devotee:

Do you still have emotions like anger?

BABA:

Ah! That is a secret. I have to act angry; otherwise people presume I do not! There is no greed or anger. There are normal people, good-hearted people, and curious people, but there are also wicked people who want to use me as a market commodity. If there is someone becoming wicked at the ashram, I need to handle it because it upsets people. I try to imagine in my mind that there is actually a problem, and then deal with it.

Devotee:

What is your knowing about how we came to be here in body form?

BABA:

No, it is only an illusion. You are actually all-pervading. When and how this happened, there is no real answer for humanity. A sadhak, one who is taking the path of meditation, is advised not to consider this because it is mind-boggling. Just focus on the goal of receding the mind because life is so precious. One can only understand this when the mind goes into deep samadhi. Our job is simply to alert you to the fact that you're just watching a movie and you're not really involved.

Devotee:

Is telling yourself that the mind is not involved simply a tactic?

BABA:

It is the Ultimate Reality. The current and ultimate reality is one and the same.

Following this question, there was a deeply touching moment, as one devotee described her grief at her father passing away and how this did not feel like imagination. In a soothing, empathetic manner, Baba explained that the mind had imagined the body of a father and that the grief is due to the imagination.

BABA:

The spiritual view says that the grief is imagination. However, the potency of imagination with grief is so strong that unless one has done Tapas, then one cannot see that illusion. The potency of a simple dream or a movie is so strong that it can affect the mind for a long time.

Devotee:

Can Baba explain some more about how it is a blessing to be born into a human body, because only then can one control the mind?

BABA:

Yes, other creatures live by instinct. Humans have thinking capacity. They can think and analyze that something is wrong in their mind. It is a rare opportunity to apply wisdom and discriminate again and again.

Devotee:

There are pictures of Swamiji meditating on deer and tiger skins. I am a vegetarian and cannot understand how these skins can be associated with meditation. How could they help with meditation?

BABA:

I do not recommend such skins. All one needs is mind control and practice. These have all been historically, traditional things. A sage has never personally taken a skin to meditate. In ancient times, people were not as greedy as today. Instead of taking just a few flowers from a tree, today people will pluck all the flowers or bananas and leave the tree bare. In ancient times the royal and hunting clan used to do hunting. They were not greedy poachers. They knew how to maintain the ecological balance. In present day situations when humans have become greedy poachers of all the animal wealth. It is not at all good to use any type of skins for meditation, which is not necessary at all. It was a practice around the world and India also to use an animal skin around their body or as a spread to sit down on the ground. Probably it was just to keep themselves warm. To get realized you can sit on a gunny-bag and do meditation.

Devotee:

Once someone gets into meditation, should they continue ritualistic worship?

BABA:

Once you get to a certain stage, it can be dropped if you like. God won't mind because the purpose of the rituals has been reached. The purpose of rituals is to prompt focus and concentration.

Devotee:

Can Baba talk a little about attachment, detachment and fear?

BABA:

The mind says, "This is me," and attachment starts. The mind is the trouble. In childhood we begin to look at everything as 'me'. It is so difficult to remove something once it is put into a child's mind. When you see God everywhere, then there is no attachment and you lose your fear as you lose attachment.

Devotee:

What is the role of prayer?

BABA:

Prayer is an effective exercise for mind control. Prayer is effective when there is total faith and the mind is not wavering. When the mind is not distracted, then it goes introverted and touches the Divine. Grace then automatically flows. If you don't imagine anything at all, having no resolutions, the inner Guru will automatically start to suck you in. Be determined, and practice; have no fear. Then, like a drop of water, you will go back to the ocean.

Devotee:

What is the balance between attachment and involvement, both emotionally and energetically?

BABA:

If there is involvement of the mind, then there is attachment.

Devotee:

I am involved in community activities and feel like I am doing something meaningful to change quality of life. Is this a good thing?

BABA:

Yes, in this world it is a good thing. But, gradually, rise above this level to become unattached. Raise your mental level above that thinking and see the Divine everywhere.

Devotee:

My mind constantly struggles when I try to meditate. What is the technique? How do I surrender?

BABA:

Ah! The mind imagines it is struggling but this is another imagination. It is a trick of the mind! It creates more impressions and you can lose half an hour of meditation like this! Keep practicing.

Devotee:

What is true religion?

BABA:

If you love, you are religious. Truly religious people consider the needs of others. They consider the need for peace to others and the world as they would consider their own need for peace. Swamiji always taught that religion is a very misunderstood word. Religious exercises are for the purpose of achieving mental, physical, and moral health. The highest value of moral health is a state in which we show consideration for others. Yogis live for others. They are for the entire humanity. It is important in spiritual growth that we show respect for all religions and all of our brothers and sisters in the world.

Devotee:

Could You please speak more about the fear of Guru and God?

BABA:

This is a satvic fear, a good fear. It does not mean we are suppressed or depressed. The fear becomes transformed into reverence to the Guru and God. It is like when you were a child; you had respect for your elders, your teachers and that fear, that respect, made you afraid to cultivate bad habits. So, the fear of elders made one think, "Oh, I should not smoke, I should not drink," and so on. Along with this, there is another quality referred to as shyness. It is also a satvic quality. It makes one shy to do the wrong thing. This gives one a reverence and seriousness in what one does. One becomes aware of one's karma, one's actions.

Devotee:

When we pray to God and ask for an answer, for guidance on a particular matter, how do we know how to recognize the answer?

BABA:

The answer will come from within. You have to recognize it coming from within. But if the mind is confused or agitated, it won't notice this inspiration from within.

Devotee:

In reading the stories of Krishna's life, it is sometimes difficult to understand His actions, as He sometimes appears to trick people, as though He is behaving badly.

BABA:

Yes, when one reads of Krishna in the *Mahabharata*, some doubt the way He handled things. Nowadays politics is so corrupted and is seen as a very bad thing. He was looking at the larger cause. Krishna had to deal with all sorts of people. Some people were cunning but had an appearance of being very nice and good, so He couldn't point out their cunningness. So, to deal with them, one has to become like them. It is like with Karna. Krishna directs his disciple Arjuna to kill Karna when he had become incapacitated. His chariot wheel was stuck in the mud, which in the usual rules of war in those days was not correct. So Karna declares to Krishna, "You are teaching adharma (wrong behavior)!" To this Shri Krishna replies, "Where was your dharma (correct behavior) when Abhimanyu was attacked by eight people, all at the same time, in the trap formation of the army? You shot him from behind, against the rules of war. Now you speak of adharma when it suits you."

So Krishna was teaching that the purpose of the act is very important. For instance, if by telling a lie, ten lives are saved, then it might be okay. If by telling the truth, ten lives are lost, this might not be good. So lying for your own good is wrong, but if genuinely trying to help society at large, then it may be right. This dharma is difficult to cover completely. It is a very wide subject. There are three aspects to it: we should look after the physical body's health with the right food and exercise; we should look after the mental aspect, by meditation and bhakti, devotion. These two are easy to understand. But the third one, the moral health, is the most difficult thing to understand—the judgment of right and wrong. Generally one will find that the people who make the rules of morality, make them to suit themselves. So in this way, Karna was sometimes tricky and cunning in his behavior; but when he was in trouble, he said another's behavior was wrong because it didn't suit him. So Krishna's behavior was not cunning, though it can appear that way at first. One has to understand His situation to grasp what He was trying to achieve and teach.

Devotee:

I read that Shri Ramana Maharshi seemed to imply that everything
in life has been decided by prarabdha karma. Does that include day-
to-day action also? In that case, wouldn't my past karma lead me to
advance spiritually without putting in effort in the present? Or is it
that my past karma provides me the opportunity to decide on the
present at every moment? In other words, can I, as a human being,
decide on the present course of action even though my past karma
puts me in various pleasant and not so pleasant situations all along
in life? Should someone work on his/her karma continuously and
accumulate positive karma with complete attention, to qualify for
spiritual advancement? Or irrespective of karma, if someone works
on thought, ego and mind, is he/she ready to advance spiritually?

BABA:

Prarabdha karma is not simply based on the karmas (actions),
but on the imprints that the mind acquires in the course of your
actions. It is these acquired habits of the mind, which form prarabdha.
So, more than the action itself, it is the impressions of the mind
which really matters. These acquired habits of the mind are known
as samskaras. Sadhana is taught so that mind may get cleansed. After
that, mind would not notice anything. Simply actions would take
place and results are accepted silently by the mind. It is when this
mind gets agitated that it experiences happiness and unhappiness.
This answer fits for your second question also, that it is the mind
and its imaginations (like ego, etc.) that you have to take care of.
Action is influenced by the mind's imaginations. If you can keep the
mind under control, gradually your actions would become more and
more noble, with a larger cause in mind, however it is not easy to
conclude anything.

Devotee:

The perception that the world is real rather than illusion, is this
of my own making or is it the collective making of mankind? Why is

mankind made to go through all this suffering along with an occasional pleasure here and there?

BABA:

It is up to the mind to see illusion or Reality. The idea of illusion is taught so that mind loses imaginations of happiness and unhappiness, and gains Supreme Peace beyond these dualities. Through logic or any other means you cannot conclude about the illusion of this world. That is why one man's food is another's poison. The world would appear to you based on the habits of the imaginations of your mind. A Yogi is only a witness and does not imagine good or bad, right or wrong, happiness or unhappiness. You need to understand this very carefully. I am talking of thought and not actions. As far as this world is concerned, if this were to be a dream or illusion, all your actions would be illusion. For instance, if there is injustice to you, you try to defend yourself. Here, if one is illusion, the other is also. Somebody doing injustice to you and you trying to defend, both are illusions (for the mind).

These things are not easy to adopt into the mind. It requires lot of austerities and Tapas practice. Otherwise, the mind is used to going into imaginations and does not stop until Nirvikalpa Samadhi is achieved, by practice and efforts.

Devotee:

Do other beings, such as plants, trees and animals go through this process too? Is there a karma attributed to their actions?

BABA:

Plants and animals also have consciousness in the form of instincts and other senses, through which the consciousness of the soul absorbs karmas. Here it is not necessary that one should be engaged in karmas to acquire prarabdha. Simply by observing others' karmas, one would absorb prarabdha (imprints). Even by watching a movie also one might acquire prarabdha imaginations, which carry on into the next birth. That is how the next birth is determined, based on the intensity of the thoughts.

Devotee:

The process of spiritual advancement seems abstract and appears to work on trust completely, especially when I read about rebirth and past karma. One cannot know or experience it unless the effort is complete. All one can do is to learn from the lives of spiritual masters and their teachings to reaffirm one's faith. Is it a bad beginning already when someone has this line of thought?

BABA:

It is not necessary that one would learn only through others' teachings or scriptures. The best learning may come from within, by inspiration, like it happened for great Ramana and Buddha. As a child, I used to get peculiar feelings that if there were some technology to switch off this entire universe, there would be the real peace of existence.

Devotee:

I have heard of teachers with occult powers who control their devotees. This makes me afraid of the spiritual path, and afraid to offer any service to a Guru.

BABA:

I promise, really, there is no such thing as occult power. What is required of any human being is a strong willpower. Also what really matters is your sincerity, your ability to decide what you actually want. If you have a strong will power, nobody can make you follow anything against your free will. If your needs are God and spiritual wisdom, naturally you will look for them, and anything else will make you uncomfortable.

When you render service to the cause of a Yogi's mission (like our Swamiji's), either with money or in any other way, depending on the devotional bhava (the quality of devotion, the attitude of the devotee), you will naturally be blessed by fruits according to the bhava of your devotion. For example, if one had aspired to worldly name and fame, status, money etc., such a devotee will be blessed in this way. This happens due to the Automatic Divine Activity, with worldly things. But these are temporary and will make the devotee more egotistic. The devotee will eventually lose a rare chance to get liberated from the worldly bondage of birth and death, craving and discontentment, dualities of happiness and unhappiness, etc.. When you render services to the cause of a Yogi's mission with selfless, sincere devotion to God, spiritual truths, and Self-Realization, you may not get that worldly name and fame during your lifetime. But you will be blessed with the Ultimate Truth, though this path may be more difficult than the one we have mentioned previously. The Divine Guru tests severely for sincerity and determination. Ultimately one will be blessed with the truth and Self-Realization. If one follows the path advocated by the Guru sincerely, the Truth shall be revealed. If one is ready to become a fool, there are people ready to fool them. Fear has no place on the spiritual path of sincere devotion. The wicked can only harm our worldly possessions and this physical body. They cannot know or touch the Immortal Soul that we really are.

Devotee:

I notice that the mind has complete control over one's senses and one has little or no control over them. Should someone have complete control over all sensory pleasures before starting on the journey of spiritual enlightenment? How can that be controlled when someone is a beginner and is so raw when it comes to spirituality?

BABA:

When mind has control over sensory organs, you try to have control over mind. Mind is your conscious energy. Sadhana is the answer. In the beginning, if it is difficult, this is no problem. Even though it is very, very difficult, it is not impossible. Somewhere you have to begin. Be determined, dedicated, disciplined and have patience. It will pay one day. Have positive thoughts that you are going to do it! Effort is worthy until the last breath of life.

Devotee:

Please explain the path of service.

BABA:

This is called Karma Yoga. Normally whatever we do, we do for ourselves. When we try to serve God and Guru, still there can be the thought of, "I am doing this." So on the path of service, we must be careful about false pride. When doing service, then surrender is very important. Do it simply as a duty, with no expectations. The mind will not allow you to do anything, except that it is always expecting something. But we need to lose these expectations. Along the path, we eventually even need to lose the desire for liberation. Then liberation itself can occur. Service can be in any form, but you need to lose pride and ego. When I first came to the ashram in Dehradun, I thought I would be simply meditating most of the time, but my Guru taught me to be ready to do anything in the ashram—clean toilets, office work, or whatever. Do it as a duty, with no expectation. Keep on doing things as you are told to, without questioning. The best service we can do is: do it without expecting; no need to ask God for anything. He will automatically give. There is no need to have expectations. God gives everything. Serve everyone as God, and then you will see God everywhere. Always offer service to God. Baba is able to love everyone because Baba sees God in everyone. Surrender and service go together. When you are ready to serve you must surrender.

Devotee:

Can You give any clues on integrating peace into our busy lives?

BABA:

When you meditate, through meditation, the mind recedes. When you get up from the meditation, the mind will remain calm. You'll be able to use the mind more effectively and you can control the mind. If you meditate, then the mind automatically gains that ability. So you can use meditation as the blanket remedy to be used in the everyday life.

Devotee:

Could You please speak about shame?

BABA:

To do a wrong thing is a shameful act. But it can be difficult sometimes to tell what a shameful act is. Generally an act, which harms one physically, mentally, or morally, is considered a shameful act. It can be easy to see a physical harm, and even mental harm. The ancient sages said that the mind can take different shapes—greed, anger, attachment, excessive stinginess, jealously and false pride. Whenever the mind gets too much into any of these shapes, your own mind is the first casualty. When this happens there is moral damage. We humans are selfish. We have one set of rules for us and another for others. When moral values are lost, we commit shameful acts. Be considerate about others. If you want to be happy, then others also want to be happy too. Greed and hatred make us selfish, and we commit shameful acts and destroy others. We should be careful about our own minds so as not to become greedy.

Devotee:

Could You please discuss the concept You mentioned 'Knowledge Personified'?

BABA:

When you reach that stage, you do not remain a separate entity from the knowledge. Usually the knowledge one has about something is like holding a chocolate in your hand. You may describe it in great detail, but you still don't know its taste. In the same way, people may think that if they read scriptures about God, they will know— but if you experience That, you become one with It. When I wanted to know myself, this 'I' vanished and only one single Self exists. If the intelligence is used to trying to know something, the intelligence is a very small thing.

Shri Ramakrishna used to tell a story about two brothers who were sent by their father to a Self-Realized master to learn about God. When they came back, he asked the first son, "What have you learned?" The son spoke at great length about all the things he had read and heard all the slokas he could recite. His father said, "Oh, you don't know anything." Then when he asked the second son, that son simply remained quiet. So the father said, "Oh good, you know a little of it." If you want the knowledge, you must experience the Truth. Swamiji used to say, "You have to experience the Truth." As a student, I didn't know much. Now as a Yogi, I can know something of why He did what He did with us. To know, to understand a Yogi, you have to become a Yogi.

Devotee:

What is a Yogi?

BABA:

Devotees have often approached me with this question, "Who is a Yogi?" You may come across saints, philosophers, spiritual leaders, the kindhearted and compassionate, but very rarely and only if you are destined, do you come across a Yogi. Yoga means: in union. Yogi is the one who has achieved it. One has to do Tapas. For me, here Tapas means: putting into the fire which consumes. What is it that you have to put into the fire, and what is that fire?

Every imagination of the mind is ego. This is the thing which you put into the fire called the Self. Actually, imagination, mind and ego are connected to each other and are in fact the same. If there is imagination, there is mind; if there is mind, there is ego. These exist in the imaginary consciousness and are thus, simply an illusion. You put this into the fire called the Self. The immortal substance that exists, the Self, shall consume this ego imagination. To achieve this you concentrate on the Self. Yes! This is what you shall be doing when you try to meditate. Meditation in its highest pitch is Tapas.

Devotee:

Just now, when we were watching the video on Baba's life, You were here next to the screen, sitting on the dais. It seemed confusing, because the mind would more easily flip over to watch the video, even though Baba Himself is directly in front of us.

BABA:

Yes, visual impact is very strong. It attracts the mind strongly. In the same way as you experienced this, God is in your heart, yet your mind is attracted out to this cinema which we call 'the world'. It is like the old expression, "We have curd at home, but go looking for butter everywhere".

Devotee:

Could You please discuss permanency and impermanency?

BABA:

The ancient sages tried to find real knowledge. They asked, "Do we last?" They found that when we watch, the consciousness gets sucked very strongly into the movie, which is called 'the real world'. Then the consciousness cannot be attentive to the Self. Spiritually, we cannot depend on this world for happiness. Be alerted about this. To be truly happy, we need to go back to the Real Self— permanent, unchanging and immortal. Consciousness always exists. The mind has come out of the Real Self, just like the ray has come out of the sun, and the droplet comes out of the ocean. We need to go back.

Devotee:

Is it realistic for a householder to strive for Self-Realization?

BABA:

It depends on the individual's determination and effort. It is like wanting to become Prime Minister of the country. Do you just simply daydream about it, or do you go full out to try to attain that? You need to want it! So you need to set your priorities, like when you took the trouble and time to come here today.

Devotee:

Could You please explain Your example of devotion to Swamiji and the ashram, and how that led on to Tapas?

BABA:

For the first twenty years of my life in the ashram, I was working like a householder, cleaning the ashram, doing office work, looking after children and the mentally handicapped boys and so on—but my mind was on Guru and was not attached to anything as 'mine'. Everything was done as a service. I loved the children and looked after them, did the work with care, but my mind was always on Swamiji. I kept praying to the Divine that I would realize the Self eventually. If one follows such methods, then definitely one can get it in this very life.

Devotee:

Is ego and mind the same?

BABA:

The mind's imaginations are ego. Actually, every thought of the mind is considered as an ego. As long as the mind has thoughts it cannot go back to the Self. You are that peace. Your mind is looking for peace and happiness, but it is not in this world. It is in the Self. The mind simply doesn't know the path. So, the Guru guides and tells you what you are really looking for and inspires you by telling you, "You can do it." The Guru points the way. That is why there is so much importance put on the Guru in the tradition. The famous song of Kabir says, "If God and Guru both come and stand in front of you, to whom should you prostrate first?" The song itself answers, "One should bow to the Guru first, because it is the Guru who has shown you God."

Devotee:

If there is no mind, and the Self is peace, how does ego come into existence?

BABA:

Actually, it never happened. Even in the Yoga Vasistha, finally at the end, it says, "All that I have said is an illusion itself. Just experience the Self." This is how the great teachers teach. If they teach too much, then it can just give more imaginations to the mind. More explanations lead to more imaginations, and it creates a vicious cycle. So do sadhana!

Devotee:

Of Swamiji's disciples, how many have reached as far as You, through Tapas?

BABA:

Some did Tapas and attained. There were two who completed the Tapas, but they dropped their physical bodies after Swamiji's Mahasamadhi. None are known to me to be alive now. However, there may definitely be some doing a lot of advanced meditation unknown to the outside world.

Devotee:

In a dialogue between Shiva and Parvati, I found something that I didn't understand. It says, "As senses are absorbed in heart, reach the center of the lotus." What does 'senses absorbed in the heart' mean? Patanjali also was talking of sense organs absorbed in the mind. What does it mean?

BABA:

'Senses absorbed in the heart' means: mind getting withdrawn from all its emotions and becoming single-pointed towards one target—the Self. This automatically happens through meditation. Meditation is the technology to do this. The emotions of the mind are always referred to as 'the spiritual heart'. The same thing Babaji refers to as brain's reflections, creating thoughts and visions. "Reaching the center of the lotus," means the mind getting absorbed into the Self, in Tapas. In old terminology, "In the center of the spiritual heart is located the lotus in which is seated the Divine— Ultimate Truth, the Self." This is experienced in deep Nirvikalpa Samadhi. The same thing is referred to by Patanjali as 'senses getting absorbed in the mind'. When mind becomes totally concentrated, first all emotions are absorbed into them. At this stage, the mind becomes the simple consciousness of existence. Slowly this mind, which is now the simple consciousness of existence, gets absorbed into the Real Self, which is beyond all imaginations.

Devotee:

Could Baba please speak about the training under Swamiji, where Baba concentrated on simply doing the work without imaginations? Baba said He worked without having the thought that, "I am doing this."

BABA:

If you have love for the Guru, then you will surrender completely. Initially if the Guru told you to do something, the mind might think, "Why should I do this thing?" or "Is this a good thing for me? Will this make me happy or unhappy?" and so on. But if one surrenders totally to the Guru, then there is no thinking or analyzing about the task. Simply the mind will get stuck on the thought, "I will do this." So where usually the mind will be having thousands of thoughts, here when one surrenders, then there is only one thought. "The Guru has said to do it," or "Let this work reach the Lotus Feet of my Guru." Then when the mind has only one thought, it will begin to recede.

Devotee:

Does Baba ever get angry?

BABA:

If I do get angry, it does not mean I have lost my temper. It might be necessary for a particular purpose to appear angry with someone, but still, when I will be exercising my temper, it will be controlled— though there may be an appearance of anger to someone watching from outside. I don't lose my temper unnecessarily. It is always controlled.

If one meditates, then the mind becomes controlled, and then the mind doesn't go into shapes of anger, pride, jealousy, and so on. It is like if you control the switch, then you have control of all the lights by that. In today's society, anger is very common, too common, as the mind is not controlled by the people. If one practices Bhakti Marga and meditation, one overcomes this anger.

Devotee:

Baba, in Your everyday life, where is Your sense of presence?

BABA:

The mind is settled in the Self's existence. For instance, if this body appears to be talking, only a little part of the consciousness is attentive to the body. Otherwise the mind's attention is totally on the Self. This is a very peculiar, amazing state. It is difficult to describe. The world is so amusing to me now. Nothing really sits into the mind anymore.

Devotee:

When we sing bhajans, is it all right to feel joy?

BABA:

The joy that comes is okay. There is no harm. But one must be aware that the ultimate goal is peace. The trouble can be that when one experiences joy, then the mind can become excited, and there is then a tendency for the mind to want to jump back into the world. So joy is good during singing. Ultimately if one is listening to music, the aim should be to become quieter in the mind.

Devotee:

Can one see God through meditation?

BABA:

One has to first consider what God is. God definitely exists as an All-Pervading Spirit. The mind's Ultimate Truth is God. But people want to see God in a physical form. The truth is, just like the mind is infinite, it exists as consciousness. So, in the same way, God exists as the ultimate existence and consciousness. Then when one meditates, if one is devoted, say to Lord Shiva, when the mind has such resolutions and then becomes 100 percent concentrated, that form one was thinking of in the resolution will manifest. But ultimately the mind has to merge with God.

Devotee:

Can Baba please explain what happens to the mind at the time of death?

BABA:

It is like what happens when you meditate. When you meditate, the mind gets kicked off the brain. The brain is an amazing physical organ that gives the mind the connection to the world, to the universe. When the brain stops, when one's physical body dies, then the mind is kicked off. If it is still active, then based on the intensity of its thoughts, it will take another body in the next birth—perhaps as an animal or human depending on its nature. The more one loses one's imaginations, the quieter the mind will become. Then it is more likely to obtain a human body. With a Yogi, who is one with the Divine— in that state referred to as moksha, nirvana, liberation, when the physical body drops off, then they become one with the All- Pervading Spirit, the Supreme Consciousness.

Devotee:

Baba says, "When the mind gets kicked off the brain." Does that mean the brain has no role?

BABA:

There is no conclusive answer that can be given for the question of whether the brain has a role. The brain is active because of the mind. The mind is active in the world because of the brain. It shows its existence in the world through the brain. We need to give up this thinking. We need to give up the mind and the brain both to reach the Ultimate Truth. This is very difficult to understand. It is a very peculiar thing, very mind-boggling.

Devotee:

It is very difficult to live in this world, as people are all so materialistic in their thoughts and behavior. So it seems best to stay out of this world and society.

BABA:

To live in this world, we only need a little of the mind's energy. We are spending too much of our consciousness on living in this world. You can live like a normal person and still use much less of your consciousness on living in this world. Even now as a Yogi, I still live in this world. I still deal with this world, but only a small amount of my consciousness is applied. It is only if you don't accept the results of your actions and efforts that you lose your peace. So one can still live in this world, but one doesn't need to spend so much of the mind's consciousness in doing so.

Devotee:

Is becoming a Yogi the only way to be one with the Divine?

BABA:

Yes, the consciousness has to become one with the Divine. That is what a Yogi is. Even if one doesn't have that title, if a person is one with the Divine, then he or she is a Yogi. It is like saying the only way you can be in this room, is to be in this room. In the same way, when someone is one with the Divine, then that one is a Yogi.

Devotee:

Are not all Yogis teachers and leaders?

BABA:

No, not all Yogis are teachers or leaders. To experience the Truth is one skill, but it is a different skill to be able to bring that out into working in this world. And it is a different skill again to be able to teach it to others also.

Devotee:

What is the symbolism behind Baba's habit of bowing down to the photo of His Guru before beginning a program?

BABA:

This is called sashtanga namaskaram, which I offer at the Lotus Feet of my beloved Guru Swamiji. The sashtanga namaskaram is a prostration symbolizing complete surrender, in which the legs, arms, body, head, the sensory organs and the mind are all offered in prostration to the Guru.

Devotee:

Babaji, there are two things that You have said which puzzle me. I've heard You say that You'll pray to God for people, but being a realized being, You are God. So how can You pray for people?

BABA:

Actually, although Self-Realized, I don't claim anything. That is not proper manners. When I'm a Saint, you are all my children. I pray to God. Claiming the status of God is not the correct language and we don't do that.

Devotee:

When You see someone, do You see their soul? Does it mean You don't see their personality and emotional energies?

BABA:

We don't see these things. It is not necessary. We see only God everywhere. That's all. I love everyone. Once realized, you see only God everywhere.

Devotee: (a little girl)

What did You look like when You were five?

BABA:

Ask my Mother and other people who saw me! (*A devotee produces a photo of Babaji's family.*) Here you can see how Baba looked.

Devotee:

It was said that Babaji's shawl has shakti within it. What does this mean?

BABA:

This is the vibration power of a Saint. It brings blessings.

Devotee:

Do we choose our parents?

BABA:

One's karma comprises the acquired habits of the mind. No one knows how it all started, what the root cause is. When a child is born, it does bring with it the acquired habits from past lives. As they say, one man's food is another man's poison. The mind's habits get carried into the next birth after the body dies. When death occurs, the brain dies, and the mind is kicked off. The acquired imprints from all the experiences shall remain in the mind. That determines the next birth. That's why the company of the good and noble is recommended— satsang. Keep in the company of learned saints and acquire detachment from the bad things of this world. When there is no attachment to the world, there is final knowledge of the Self, and then you get liberated. For the last seven days I have been here, have you heard any bad things from me? Even if you don't believe everything I have said, practice for yourself and know the truth yourself.

Devotee:

What is the significance of the arati (waving the light), and why is it performed?

BABA:

The arati is a traditional way of showing supreme reverence. If a Self-Realized Master is present, then He can be seen as almost equal to God. So this is a way we have of showing our reverence. We do it at the beginning of the program and also at the end, as a proper way to start and finish the program.

Devotee:

Is there an explanation for the out-of-body experience?

BABA:

The awareness has come out in two ways. The mind comes out into the universe, while another part of it comes into the body. This part, which comes into the body, is called kundalini, the coiled energy. Of these two, the mind is much more powerful. If the mind gets concentrated, it lifts the kundalini in the body, and such experiences can occur. Actually the soul doesn't leave the body. The soul is not hidden in the body. It is just the mind lifting the kundalini that gives this sensation.

Devotee:

Why is a Guru needed? Is He superior to other people, or is it just something like people looking for a father figure?

BABA:

If the Guru has become one with the Self, is a Jivanmukta, then He is one with God. To the disciples He will look superior, but for the Guru, He simply sees God everywhere. The Guru will not see himself as superior. As one would revere God, then disciples will revere the Guru. This reverence is necessary to be serious in the practice of the meditation. Ultimately such reverence is only a recommended thing in the scriptures, it is not compulsory. It has to come from the disciples themselves. The Guru guides the students towards God. He tries to tell them there is a special purpose for this human life, beyond the day-to-day life of simply existing. Guru inspires, like a mother encouraging the children to go to school.

Devotee:

Why do so many Gurus come from India? The spiritual knowledge seems to keep coming as a chain of occurrences.

BABA:

In India, the culture itself encourages one not to have too many desires. The scriptures of India, such as the Vedas and Upanishads are very inspiring for those seeking God. Also there is a long tradition of reverence towards the Guru, so the teachings were also open to all. The saints were not killed, as in some other places, and so there was openness in teachings being heard and spread.

Devotee:

Why is it easier to meditate when Baba is physically present?

BABA:

Possibly it might be due to your attachment to Baba's physical form. So perhaps you should train yourself to feel Baba within, and stay in His vibrations, even when He is not physically present. Then you will follow Baba's teachings all the time, and won't be able to go against them. You will feel Baba always with you.

Devotee:

Why is the vibhuti used in the initiation?

BABA:

It is a traditional blessing, and can be helpful. It can help to bring you faith and devotion, which will help in the meditation. It will help you to receive the Divine Guru's grace and blessings.

Devotee:

Could Baba discuss prayers being offered for departed souls?

BABA:

This is a way to remember and honor them. This way we remember their good points, and so feel inspired to help in this world—to make it a better place. In India there is also a tradition of feeding people in the name of a departed soul. In olden days, people used to particularly feed a section of society. Those sections of people had it as their job to look after the spiritual things for the society and were always looking after everyone else. So they had no time to earn for themselves. It was a tradition at such ceremonies to feed them and give clothes also. Now that is not the case so much, so we tend to feed the people who are poor and needy. It gives tremendous satisfaction to oneself to do such things. The old Sanskrit word for this is translated as: tribute for the departed soul. But each soul must do their own sadhana. No one can do it for you. Any noble work you do is for your own self. Swamiji used to say that the tradition of reciting God's name, "Ram, Ram," when carrying a body to the funeral, that it is better to do it for yourself while still alive.

Devotee:

Are there stages in death, in dying?

BABA:

Once death occurs to the body, if the mind still has retained imprints, these make the mind take up a new body. For a Yogi, there are no desires or imaginations in the mind, so there is no need for them to take up a new body again. If the mind is violent at the time of death, then such a soul may go down, even to a lower species. But if the mind is not too violent or restless at the time of death, then such a soul gets elevated towards God. They will get the circumstances that are conducive to go towards God in the next birth.

Devotee:

Baba talks about being more selfless in our behavior, but isn't it true that we need to first experience more of our Self first, so that we have a more complete idea of who we are, before we can be more truly selfless?

BABA:

Yes, I understand your point. And this is actually how things do occur; there must be ignorance to be able to appreciate knowledge. There must be suffering, to be able to appreciate happiness and peace. In the same way, we do become very selfish initially as we grow, but then, over time, automatically it will happen that the selflessness develops. However, as a teacher it is my job to tell you to be good and selfless. It is a bit like, if I tell you not to put your hand in the fire, because if you do that you will get harmed. I could let you simply put your hand in, but then you would get hurt. So I tell you, "Don't put your hand in the fire." In the same way, I tell you to behave well, so then you won't get harmed.

Devotee:

Could You talk more about detachment?

BABA:

Detachment is not a way of turning your back on the world. It is like, if you are looking after your child—it is mainly that you are looking after your child very carefully; because of the blood relationship you have with that child. But you may not look after other children just as carefully, because the same blood relationship is not there. Now if you could look after that child just as carefully, but because you see that it is God in that child, then it will be easier for you to also look after other children in the same way. And so, in this way, your consciousness expands. You start to see God in all hearts, and in all things. It is like when I left home to go to the ashram, some family members were ridiculing me saying, "Why are you deserting your mother like this?" I simply explained that I was in the fortunate circumstance that I had two elder brothers who had agreed to look after my mother, so she would be taken care of properly. If I went to the ashram, then by serving the ashram, I would be able to serve so many mothers that came, not just the one.

Devotee:

Do those relatives who said these things when Baba was leaving to go to the ashram, now think Baba made a good choice?

BABA:

Yes, now they think it was a very wise choice. (*The audience all laughed in appreciation.*)

Devotee:

If children have grown up in difficult circumstances, how can they be shown their good side, their kind side?

BABA:

We can inspire them. For instance, with stories of people from the great epic stories, who have similarly faced difficulties and have overcome them. We can inspire them to be strong, to be brave, and to keep trying.

Devotee:

In the Christian church, there is sometimes a lot of emphasis placed on the second coming of Jesus. Could you please comment on this?

BABA:

As this is a religious question, I would ask to be excused from answering it. It would not be proper for me to comment. But what I might say is that for those people who are very attached to Jesus, then they should look for Him in their hearts. This is what Jesus himself said, "The kingdom of heaven is within you." This is what all the great saints have said also.

Devotee:

What is Baba's mind like during meditation? When I mediate, I am constantly thinking of all the things that went on during today or yesterday, but what is Baba's mind like during meditation?

BABA:

For ordinary people, the mind is constantly having thoughts. It is either brooding about the past, or worrying about the future. It is always picturizing these things as thoughts. But for my mind, there is no picturizing. It is always calm, and at peace.

Devotee:

Can a Self-realized soul perform the mundane, day-to-day tasks of the world?

BABA:

Yes, it is definitely possible. The difference is that for you, you are spending so much of your mental energy in all these things—in planning and worrying about these things. There is actually no need to use that much of your mental energy to live in this world. For me, it is now natural for my attention to be on God. So, that attention needs to be brought back to the world. Just as your attention is naturally on the world, my attention is naturally on God. To bring the attention back to the world now requires some effort on my part to bring it about. So, sometimes you'll notice me making little hand gestures or things like that, to bring the attention back to this world. To have the attention on God is one skill, and to have it able to function in this world is another skill.

Devotee:

Do the horrible things that are happening in the world, like war and other things upset you?

BABA:

No, because my view of things is different than yours. It is the long history of the world that there have always been problems like this. For 2000 years, 5000 years, perhaps for 10,000 years the Saints have been coming and trying to tell people to care for each other— to behave properly, but still people are the same. Yet, it is still worth trying to improve things. It is worth putting in the effort. Whether we succeed in changing the world is not the important thing. It is important that we simply try. It is important that we go on trying, until the last breath of life in this body. The trying is what is important. We should keep trying to teach these things until the last breath of life in this body.

In the story of Shri Rama, He comes in the war against Ravana. To take the whole monkey army over to Lanka, He needs to build a bridge to get them across the sea. So they are building the bridge from rocks and boulders. Then the squirrels also want to help. All they can do is go and roll around on the sand, so that some of the sand gets stuck to their fur, and then they bring that to the place where the bridge is being built and simply shake that sand off their backs onto the bridge, to add to the building that is going on. Rama is so amazed to see them making such efforts, and is very pleased and accepts their offering. In the same way, we cannot change the whole world, but even the very little that we can offer is offered to God and He accepts it. So in the same way, it doesn't matter if 10,000 people come to the programs which we hold, or not. Here tonight there are only twenty to thirty people, but that itself is a great thing; and so we offer that to God and simply go on.

Devotee:

In Baba's tape recorder analogy, with relation to the brain and mind, do all the impressions in the mind need to be run through the brain and watched in order to be erased?

BABA:

The brain functions as a tape recorder with the mind as the tape. Countless impressions and experiences of a life are recorded in the mind—until they can be released and purified by means of sadhana, especially the sadhana of meditation. During meditation, the mind gets applied on the brain, and the brain de-codifies the acquired habits recorded in the mind. In this subtle purification process, thoughts and images, sights and sounds, are shown to the meditator. If watched with alert attention as a witness, but without attachment or analysis, these can be erased and evaporated from the mind. Otherwise, if the meditator attaches to these thoughts, sights or sounds or judges and analyses them, these same impressions or imaginations are re-absorbed by the brain and again recorded in the mind.

Yes! All the acquired habits of the mind would get erased by going through this process of the brain creating visions and thoughts. It's a tricky situation you cannot conclude—but still this is what happens when one is able to observe closely. This continues up to a stage, as long as the mind does not get de-linked totally from the brain—to go to samadhi. Visions and thoughts—sight and sound is what I would like to call these—in different potencies will continue. First, like imaginations and then, when the mind's concentration increases in advanced meditation, mental projection happens. Finally, at the height of Tapas, when the mind would have achieved total concentration, but still some residue of resolutions remain— manifestations, including the form of God coming in front of the sadhak, and so on happen. After this manifestation (of the form of God), a peculiar vision happens. It appears as if that deity, that form of God, will be merging in you, where as actually, it is the mind, which merges with the Self. That is when the Nirvikalpa Samadhi occurs. I suppose, when only an awareness of existence remains and Supreme Peace is there. It is not necessary that every sadhak getting realized will undergo this type of mental projections and manifestations. It would totally depend on the acquired habits of the mind of such a person who is going into Tapas. Many may not simply observe these things happening. All the manifestations or projections may go unnoticed or ignored. By a peculiar illusion, the mind and brain have come together and exist because of the other. Mind is the main petrol for the brain and the brain is the main petrol for the existence of the mind. A sadhak has to skillfully try to de-link the mind, without trying to affect the health of the brain.

Devotee:

When watching the mind in meditation, it seems that the mind comes to stillness. If the mind becomes still, how do impressions then continue to be erased, if they aren't arising. It seems that once we've become lost in thinking again, it's due to becoming somewhat unconscious and ceasing to watch. In that way one is caught up again and the brain isn't getting purified. Would impressions then be absorbed back into the mind? This point gets a little discouraging because sometimes I realize I've been off on a series of thoughts without realizing it, for far more time than I've been watching.

BABA:

This is a wonderful question. When it appears to you that the mind has become still, it would be for a while only. Thinking arises because mind has not yet got rid of its acquired habits. Once it starts thinking, unknowingly, it is acquiring further impressions. Because, when the mind is rid of all the impressions and is totally purified, the thoughts would not arise, and a permanent stillness occurs which is samadhi—Supreme Peace and awareness of existence. It is because of becoming unconscious (ceasing to watch), and getting absorbed into thoughts, that the mind's attention is again on the illusion of its own imaginations. That's where the tricky thing is. When thoughts come, try to ignore. It would not be possible to make out which is the thought and which is analyzing that thought. Both would appear as a thought only. When thoughts come, do not get discouraged or irritated. It should be like a sports game, playing for the championship—a duel battle for the valiant soldier. You should enjoy fighting it out. Try and ignore thoughts; that is the best weapon that you have. Then the opponent thought will get beaten up.

Devotee:

When the mind has been completely purified, does one experience pure consciousness as a state completely independent of the brain or any physical reflector? Is it only pure awareness, which can recognize itself as itself? If so, what is the role of the brain, after the mind has been completely purified of all impressions? At this stage, is mind only the Self and not reflected by the brain? Why would pure awareness then stay in touch with that individual brain?

BABA:

When the mind is completely purified, it would be absorbed into the Self—completely independent of the brain; it is Supreme Peace—pure awareness of existence. Only this pure awareness can recognize the Self, its own Self, because there are no more imaginations. Still it exists as Pure Consciousness or Awareness. Concerning the role of the brain, now the tables have turned upside down. As long as the imaginations were there, the brain was behaving like a Master, making the mind to dance to its tunes. Whatever it reflected, the mind took in good faith and believed it as the truth. But now the brain has become the servant and the mind—because of getting absorbed into the Self—is the Master. The mind uses the brain to help others to go on this path and get Realized. It uses the brain and is fully aware that whatever is being done is simply an imagination.

Just like teachings of the Guru, the Self is aware that it is using the brain to imagine—to teach for the sake of understanding only and it is not the total truth. The Guru, the Self, is just giving clues to inspire the student to pursue seriously, until the student gets rid of all the imaginations. The actual Truth is only when you experience it. Remember what Sage Vasistha tells Rama at the end of the discourse, "Hey Rama, whatever was told by me all these days as discourse of the Ultimate Truth is also an imagination." Just be there and experience the Truth. Nothing else is the Truth. The Yogi's Truth is the Self and is not reflected by the brain.

Devotee:

Do these same principles of watching and purifying the mind happen in daily activity if one is alert to the Self while performing activity? Or is activity a time of gathering more impressions, which then need to be released during meditation? There are times in activity when I notice everything becomes very still and perception becomes grainy, as if unreal and dissolving. At these times is the mind being purified or are we taking in further impressions, even if subtle?

BABA:

The same principle of watching and purifying the mind does happen, if one is alert. The same principle works on the path of devotion also—surrender. After putting in efforts, when results come, they shall be accepted as the Divine's wishes. The mind shall remain quiet without brooding, missing, or expecting anything, or making analyzations and judgments. In the same way, when the Guru is physically around, if one can simply accept what Guru teaches and do not bother to analyze what Guru does—if the mind simply accepts, the same principle works. This normally happens naturally, when one falls in love with the Guru unconditionally.

Devotee:

During a recent meditation, I realized there has always been part of my mind in which I 'try to be good'. This part tries to figure out 'the rules' and then abide by them, as if my safety and success depended on it. This occurs primarily in my spiritual life, as I would try to learn what the Guru wanted of me and then carry out his orders. But it wasn't really carrying out his orders in loving seva, but a seeking for my own security and understanding—that if I did things 'the right way' I would be safe and protected. Somehow I realized last night that this was ego, just ego. I also felt Swamiji was the inspiration for this realization, that His personality is one that brings us to freedom, not to being good—that Ardhanarishwara is too free, too wild, to be held in a container of the mind. And if I want to know Him/Her then I needed to somehow break this neediness.

BABA:

Mind wants to be holding on to the dualities of either of the two—either the good or the bad. Rejecting bad or good is simply imagination. There is neither good nor bad. One Self exists and the sadhak shall not try to define it in any way. Just become quiet. When a real experience of the Self occurs, there is tranquilized quietness. No definitions are there because mind has been absorbed into the Self. Swamiji is the Self. You are right that the mind needs to break neediness.

Devotee:

This morning I sat to meditate and put my attention on bhrikuti. I realized that energy was pulling the attention up. In the past I had never allowed the attention to follow but 'clung' to bhrikuti in order to be a 'good' meditator as per my understanding of Dhyana instructions. This morning I surrendered to the energy. I went right up and into ajna chakra and the mind became still. Waves of thoughts and sounds came in at times, but I was on top of them, like a log floating on ocean waves. Eventually energy went up to the crown and there was an opening that reminded me of the way a planetarium roof spirals open—also like the way a vegetable steamer spirals open. Then it was still—ananda. There was still some thought 'below' and body awareness. But the body was felt without pleasure or pain duality, so it was bliss energy rather than dumb matter. What the mind calls pain in knees, etc. was experienced as shakti releasing from the body, like fire releasing from wood. When the energy got too powerful I eventually began to have thoughts and fidget. Then meditation ended.

BABA:

When this type of experience occurs, it is essential to have total detachment to the experience. Just wait—allow things to happen until consciousness called mind goes beyond this bliss, ananda, and gets de-linked from the brain—when it shall loose all locations and attention of other things. Just exist until it does not become, effortlessly being there, totally contented and gaining awareness of existence that is Supreme Peace.

Devotee:

With this technique of meditation, will it take you through the eight levels of jnana meditation?

BABA:

With this technique, there is no need to worry about different stages. It is all taken care of automatically.

Devotee:

Can You give any clue or hint as to how we can recognize our thoughts as imaginations?

BABA:

Whatever is in the mind are only imaginations. Because the mind exists only when it imagines! The pure existence of the Self is peaceful. Anything else is imagination because the mind cannot exist without thoughts. The only real experience is peace. But the mind cannot remain even on one thought. It constantly recognizes and makes judgments. When all this stops, then you experience your Existence.

Devotee:

You told me to focus attention on the spontaneous image of light that used to come very often during meditation. Recently there is little or no image of light. It feels like the light was quite blissful and has calmed down and disappeared. It reminds me of the change from piti, a thrilling sort of rapture, to sukha, a more peaceful bliss, from the second to the third jnanas. When there is no light or anything much else, what should I focus on?

BABA:

It is fine if the image of light no longer appears, just focus on the consciousness of existence. If you just keep looking to the front portion or, if possible, in between eyebrows, that will take care of consciousness of existence.

Devotee:

The Lord Buddha described how nirodha, extinction, is the ultimate happiness, Nirvana. During all of the jnanas, there is some awareness, even in the eighth jnana, neither perception nor non-perception, there is supposed to be a very subtle awareness. Isn't that awareness what allows us to feel the Supreme Peace and deep happiness? If in nirodha there is no awareness at all, how can it feel so good? Wouldn't it be like being deep in sleep, with no feelings at all?

BABA:

There could be some misunderstanding on what exactly Buddha wanted to convey. Extinction means that of the mind, which is always aware of such things, which it imagines. Awareness of the Self would be there in enlightenment but without any thoughts of 'I' or 'this' or 'that'. It is beyond all imaginations and is neither awareness nor extinction. There is Supreme Peace. If Buddha says that in extinction there is Supreme Peace, who is the one who experiences this Supreme Peace? Without existence of the Self who will be there to experience this Supreme Peace? So, 'there is Supreme Peace' means it has to be for the Self, which exists and experiences.

Devotee:

Babaji, in meditation I often drift off into nothingness, like I've been somewhere. I feel separate from my body, as if in a void.

BABA:

The soul never really travels anywhere. It remains intact and is all-pervading. When we meditate and we gain more concentration, the mind loses its imaginations and tries to lift body consciousness upwards. This body consciousness is called kundalini. This kundalini consciousness is the same substance as the mind. Before attaining samadhi, the kundalini rising can create certain sensations like a feeling of lightness, being out of the body, increase in body temperature, the illusion of traveling through space, etc. It is only the mind which has gone somewhere in its imagination. If our aim is Self-Realization and divinity, we must understand that all such experiences are illusions. The mind and kundalini get de-linked from the brain, and then later we proceed to samadhi. What you're experiencing is a sign of progress, just don't analyze what is happening. Otherwise the mind comes into existence and gets involved.

Devotee:

Please say something about eating and physical exercise before and after meditation.

BABA:

Eating is an important habit. Take some food two to three hours before meditation, so that when you sit, you feel lighter. Eating too much, too close to meditation will make you sleep. After meditation you can do some stretches and other physical exercises, or a little before. You can also do the Indian Yoga exercise called Shavasana, the corpse pose, to relax.

Devotee:

In meditation I get headaches, breathlessness and blurred vision.

BABA:

This can happen if you force things. Just watch and don't force. If these symptoms persist, check there isn't a physical problem causing these things.

Devotee:

Babaji, please tell us a story about Swamiji, Shivabalayogi Maharaj.

BABA:

Swamiji was born in a coastal town of Andhra Pradesh. He lost his father while quite young and came from a poor family. They were weavers. At five years of age, he realized his family was poor, dropped out of school and started working. He developed a business but God had other plans for this child. At the age of fourteen, in 1949, his grandfather was away in the nearby city of Kakinada for an operation to remove a cataract. Swamiji's food was being prepared by his sister. That day he felt restless. He sat outside with friends, then went to bathe in a canal nearby, had a cup of coffee and something to eat. While walking nearby, he saw some fruits falling from a tree. He picked up one of the pieces to squeeze out the juice. He heard a monotone *Om* sound coming from the fruit. He couldn't see properly because of a dazzling light, but did see that the fruit took the form of a Shivalingam, broke into two pieces and a matted-haired Sage emerged from the fruit. The Sage made Swamiji sit in the lotus position and applied vibhuti to his forehead. Swamiji immediately became absorbed into deep meditation.

Later people tried to wake him up from this meditation without success. Some thought he had become possessed by an evil spirit. Swamiji moved to the graveyard in the village, because the villagers had thrown stones at him, and even a cloth with burning kerosene. In the graveyard, his skin started to decay. It was the rainy season and he was bitten mercilessly by rats and scorpions. By nature, Swamiji was a very determined person with enormous inner strength. Nonetheless, eventually Swamiji asked himself why he should live like a dead person and felt that he should go back to work and support his mother. Before he could leave the graveyard, the same Sage re-appeared and told Swamiji that he was going to do Tapas for twelve years and that after finishing he would be free to go anywhere he liked. Still Swamiji wondered whom the person was who had made him to sit. On being asked, the Sage replied that despite all that he had done for Swamiji, he still didn't know who he was!

At the end of the twelve years, a dazzling male-female form of Shiva and Parvati appeared to Swamiji, spoke to him and said he was free to go. Swamiji said he had no wish other than what they wanted him to do. He was instructed to initiate every human being who wanted to come to him—without regard to caste or creed.

They said that human beings need to know who they are, truly. They then merged into his body. For thirty-three years Swamiji carried out this mission, traveling to the UK, USA, Sri Lanka and elsewhere, teaching this meditation and the philosophy of Yoga Vasistha. Swamiji spoke very little and emphasized practice and sadhana. May you all be inspired to do this sadhana.

Devotee:

Babaji, could You please explain the relationship between Nirvikalpa Samadhi, Self-Realization, liberation from physical life, and liberation from all life?

BABA:

Nirvikalpa Samadhi is the state in which the mind is totally absorbed in the Self. All imaginings are lost, even the 'I' thought. The mind has settled in the Self effortlessly and naturally. When Self-Realization occurs, the mind has also been absorbed into the Self, the All-Pervading Ultimate Truth of Existence. The mind—which until that point has defined, analyzed and judged—finally loses its imaginations and returns to the source of real existence. Self-Realization can happen while the physical body is alive, so one is mentally liberated. The term for this is Jivanmukta. A Jivanmukta is one who is liberated while still alive in the physical body. One can also reach the Divine and be liberated when the physical body is dropped. This is known as Videhamukti. Jivanmukta means that only a minimal amount of consciousness is in touch with the brain and doesn't acquire future prarabdha karma. The Yogi's mind does not have imaginings or cravings, but remains the active witness and is not involved. Your mind, however, does not keep quiet, and exists in its own world. Losing the physical body is not liberation. The mind must lose its imaginations before liberation can occur. A Yogi's mind has no imaginations. Even the thought, "I have the body," doesn't occur. The Yogi's mind is merged into pure consciousness.

Devotee:

What is the Guru's role?

BABA:

A Guru is the one who shows the path. The Guru gives clues how to proceed, and inspires by inducing faith. What I have achieved, you can also achieve. A disciple must authorize the Guru to train him or her—just like a surgeon is authorized by the patient to do an operation. The more you can authorize the Guru, the better it is, but this can be a bitter experience at times. The student should have total faith and should surrender to the Guru. The Guru is the one who dispels the darkness of ignorance—this is what the word actually means in Indian philosophy. *Guru Brahma, Guru Vishnu, Gurudevo Maheshwara.* This sloka means that the Guru is a form of the Divine; the Divine is your Guru.

Devotee:

If a person is very sick, pain-filled, and can't concentrate, is it better to meditate in this painful state? Does it burn up karma?

BABA:

Put in effort. A doctor keeps trying to help his very ill patients—so just keep trying; there is no harm in this, even though it may be very difficult.

Devotee:

What is the benefit to westerners singing bhajans if they don't know Sanskrit?

BABA:

It is normal practice to sing the glory of God and Guru. If a person can sing soothingly, with devotion and faith to the Deity or Guru, this will help concentration. The mind touches the Divine, so Divine grace flows automatically. That's why we pray. Concentration is achieved through devotion and faith. Music can assist in mind control. It's not really necessary to know the meanings of all the words. One hundred percent faith will see you through to reach God-Consciousness.

Devotee:

Babaji, I work at a university, and there I feel I need defenses in such a negative environment. Yet I also want to renounce all that is not good. But then how can I live in the world and make money?

BABA:

To be virtuous, you don't need to be a fool. You need to be clever and diplomatic. You don't need to sacrifice virtue to make money. Remember the story of the Saint and the snake. One day a Saint was passing through a village and saw a poisonous snake. The Saint advised the snake to be noble and remember God and then went away. As the snake was very much impressed by the Saint's vibrations, it resolved to follow the advice of the Saint. The next day when the village urchins came it kept quiet, thus the children were not afraid to come close to the snake. Still when the snake was quiet, one of them threw a small stone. The snake did not react. Then the urchins thought, "This snake is harmless. We can do anything with it." Assuming thus, they went on throwing more and more stones. By this, the snake got seriously injured and was bleeding very much. A couple of days later when the Saint came back, he wanted to see the snake, whether it is following his advice or not. When he saw the snake, he asked, "What is this? Who has hurt you like this?" The snake replied, "Venerable, Saint, because I tried to follow your advice to remain noble and good to others, this is my condition now." The Saint merely replied that he had instructed only that it should be noble and not hurt anyone; this didn't mean the snake couldn't do a bit of hissing to threaten his attackers away! Likewise, in your job in the world, you have the right to defend yourself. As Krishna also taught—if war is declared, then one may have to respond with equal force, to defend oneself. But, one should keep the mental level free from hatred and revenge.

Devotee:

What is the relationship between the mind and love?

BABA:

Love is seeing God everywhere. Love doesn't expect anything. The mind expects something. It cannot keep quiet. Don't expect results. That is mind control—not brooding, but staying contented always. I love you all even if you do not love me!

Devotee:

Is that why we find it so easy to love You? You're the easiest to love!

BABA:

That is good! If you love Baba, you will be benefited. In all my programs, I try to brain wash you all the time (*laughing*). You will be able to receive. A Yogi's vibrations are always flowing. With faith and love you can catch them. Shri Ramakrishna used to tell a story about a Guru who had a student and a maidservant. The maidservant had absolute faith in the Guru. There were floods in the area, and while crossing the river, she repeated his name with absolute faith and made it to the other side of the river safely. But the student had doubts about the effectiveness of the Guru's name, and so was carried away by the current and drowned. Such is the power of love and devotion. The moral of the story is that it's up to you to make the most out of the love you automatically receive from the Guru.

Devotee:

When I meditate my body gets hot and I get distracted. What causes this?

BABA:

Mental concentration causes the kundalini or consciousness to rise. This kundalini is the same substance as the mind. A sadhak shouldn't be concerned about the kundalini. Heat is produced as the consciousness within the kundalini is distributed in the body.

Devotee:

How do you know if you're making progress on the path?

BABA:

When you achieve more peace of mind, when agitations decrease, and the mind gives up its habits of brooding. If you are overly psychologically sensitive and brood over upsets and criticism, say for weeks at a time, meditation will shorten this.

Devotee:

I have a significant struggle between a blissful, virtue-filled reality, and my own experience being a householder and someone who works. What you describe seems so far from my world. There is so much pain.

BABA:

As you continue to practice, try to help others who are in pain. Do it as a duty, but without attachment to the results. Otherwise, your mind will experience frustration. The Ultimate Truth is the Self. Nothing can affect the Self. A Yogi remains unperturbed, yet we have compassion. All is a play of the Divine. Nothing can disturb the real existence of the soul. In the Bhagavad-Gita, Krishna teaches that one shouldn't get mentally attached to one's actions. Swami Vivekananda taught that if you get too involved and perform actions with attachment, you'll have expectations, and experience pain, longing and disappointment when these expectations aren't met. Everyone is playing a role. There is ultimately neither good nor bad. Practice meditation, it will help you to keep detached and experience the play as though it were a movie. Think that God is everywhere, and that it is your job to play your role. Everything is ultimately under God's control. It's not our job to judge people. Just help people and surrender.

Devotee:

Babaji, sometimes when I meditate I feel like I'm on fire. What is happening?

BABA:

This can happen. When the mind becomes more concentrated,

the conscious energy is spread in the body. This is what is also called 'the raising of the kundalini'. Don't worry. Drink some water. Keep concentrating the mind.

Devotee:

Is that why you should have a Guru, to become involved in meditation?

BABA:

A child needs a mother. A disciple needs a Guru, who imparts knowledge and wisdom. The Guru protects, inspires, and encourages seriousness on the part of the disciple. The Guru is the one who dispels the darkness of ignorance. It is because of ignorance that troubles occur. This is why the Guru is considered vital in Indian philosophy. He is considered equal to God, *Guru Brahma, Guru Vishnu, Gurudevo Maheshwara, Guru Sakshat Para Brahma.* The Guru is one who has attained Jivanmukti and can guide you towards enlightenment. As the great Saint Kabir said, "If God and the Guru both appear before me, who should I prostrate to first? The Guru, because it is the Guru who told me about God." There is a difference between knowledge and wisdom. Knowledge is like knowing how to fire a gun, but wisdom is knowing when to fire it! The Guru is the one who can give the highest truth to the disciple.

Devotee:

A friend of mine died this morning. He didn't believe in God or any teaching. What happens to a soul like that?

BABA:

Purity and peacefulness are more important than beliefs. If the mind is non-violent and peaceful, free from hatred, it is good. True religion means keeping the mind under control, and the body disciplined and healthy, as well as adhering to moral values. These factors determine the quality of the next life.

Devotee:

My question is about pain. How does a person begin to overcome painful and traumatic events?

BABA:

Keep free from hatred. You'll at least be elevated. There are six shapes of the mind: extreme greed, anger, stinginess, attachment to material things, jealousy, and false pride. When the mind takes the shape of these things, it loses its peace. If someone dislikes you, you at least must not hate them, otherwise you'll be the first casualty.

Devotee:

What is the ego and how do we acquire it? Why do we need to lose it?

BABA:

Every imagination of the mind is ego. Greed, anger, likes, dislikes, false pride, jealousy, all these are ego, as well as craving and mental habits. Egos clash with each other. Countries have fought wars over tiny pieces of land, because of the egos of their leaders. We should try to find our own faults. The problem is that we have falsely identified the body as the Self. The ego troubles the mind. It analyzes, judges, interprets, and so on. Once someone accused Buddha of wrong doing. He merely said, "You gave me a gift just now, I'll give it back to you. If you meditate regularly, you'll be able to lose the ego and experience the Real Self as the Immortal Soul that exists beyond the body." We have forgotten the Self, like being so totally absorbed in a movie, that we forget we're actually just watching it.

Devotee:

Is it necessary to do Tapas to become Realized?

BABA:

Yes, but Tapas also includes Bhakti Marga, the devotional path. Tapas means that the consciousness should be on the Self-Realization or God-realization. In the story of Mirabai, she had such devotion to Lord Krishna that only Krishna existed for her. She saw him everywhere. For her, it became her Tapas. True bhakti is not about just waving incense sticks, but the consciousness must be on the

Deity. This is also Tapas. Ultimately you'll have to do Tapas.

Devotee:

You've spoken about Your relationship with Your Guru, and some of the light-hearted and serious moments with Swamiji. Please tell us more!

BABA:

Swamiji was compassionate like a mother, yet he was also tough like a father. He would never compromise on spiritual teachings, sadhana, or work. At times He got annoyed, but even this was for the purpose of teaching something or to train us. Just like someone is taught to swim by being dropped in the water, then watched and rescued if necessary. One day, early in the morning at around 3:30, I was to bring Swamiji His milk. Swamiji was very particular about time. If I was ten or fifteen minutes early, I would be nervous. This time I was two minutes late. Swamiji berated me, saying I was drinking the milk for myself. One day He took the milk and He was scolding me and shouting for forty-five or fifty minutes, while He was sipping the milk for the whole time. Then He laughed, saying there was an evil spirit dancing on the top of my head, and that He was trying to scare him away! Then Swamiji gave me some sweets. Everyday at meditation I used to bring Him and escort Him onto the dais, and every tea time I used to go to His room. I would fill up His water jug, keep His room clean, and fill up the buckets. While there, I would also eat one piece of sweets every day. One evening when Swamiji came in his room he opened the sweet box and said laughing, "Oh! Today he hasn't eaten anything!" I felt secure at His lotus feet. Swamiji would never compromise on sadhana though. He was my mother and father and Guru.

Devotee:

Babaji, please tell the story about how Swamiji made you wait outside the hall.

BABA:

It was 1978, four years after I had joined Swamiji. We were in the Bangalore Ashram. A table and some chairs were kept outside the entrance door of the hall. After arati, Swamiji asked me where I wanted to sit. He said, "Take a sweet and just keep sitting there," saying, "Let me test you." I ate the sweet and waited for Swamiji to come out of the hall, as He usually did. But he didn't come out. Hours passed. Some devotees came outside and told me that Swamiji was furious that I was still outside. Swamiji ordered them not to give me any food or water, and they told me to come inside and eat. I replied that I had promised Swamiji that I would stay where I was, and that I would not leave. Swamiji then told them not to talk to me at all! I was being bitten by mosquitoes; it was feast time for them. I kept repeating His name. More time passed. Finally at 4 o'clock, Swamiji emerged and saw me, saying, "Poor boy, I just remembered Seenu sitting there." I was nervous. Swamiji ordered that food be brought and that day Swamiji sat at the table. The whole episode was a great test of determination. Swamiji said of me, "Even if I cut him into pieces, and throw him in the river, he will get joined back together and come back to me." It is not easy to serve the Guru like that. Serving the Guru leads to the descent of God's grace. There is no difference between a Realized Yogi and God. All you need is unwavering faith. This came naturally to me. God's grace came to me in the form of Swamiji.

Devotee:

Is it possible to do Tapas and still stay in worldly life?

BABA:

Yes, it is possible. Your attitude must change though. There is a worldly life for me also; I talk, travel, and love. I don't live in forests or caves. A householder can do Tapas, if the attitude changes. His or her consideration towards others would increase and life would become a mission. It would not be a life devoted to filling one's own belly. It would be a life devoted to the welfare of others.

Devotee:

Baba, can You explain how an unborn baby can benefit from being in the presence of a Yogi; how a baby can perceive the vibrations?

BABA:

The vibrations are always there. The mother's brain will be positively affected. The baby will be able to receive blessings in the presence of a Saint.

Devotee:

How important is it to have the physical presence of a Guru?

BABA:

The presence of the Guru can inspire, because the student is likely to lose seriousness. Doubts may arise. The Guru says, "This is how you must proceed." This is the bonus of the physical presence. You can look to the Guru for inspiration. The Guru is there to correct you. We met Shivabalayogi when young, and for twenty years I was able to serve Him and learn. The next generation will learn about Him from us. Listen to what I have come to teach. The Guru teaches by his life's example. After Babaji drops his physical body, you will be able to say what he was like and what he taught.

Devotee:

What do you do if children are uncontrollable?

BABA:

Give them love, but insist—politely refuse. You have to give a lot of time to children. You are like children to me. I try to motivate you. I always say, "Forgive and forget." I try to be a friend. I try to inspire people. The present generation has been exposed to too much and is undisciplined. They consider any discipline to be slavery. Meditation will help.

Devotee:

Why does evil exist?

BABA:

The presence of evil makes the Divine's drama work. It teaches the value of good. The world consists of duality. If it wasn't for experiencing bad, we would never realize the value of good. Just like in a movie, scene after scene wicked people win, until the final scene, in which the hero is victorious. Such wicked people help God carry on His worldly drama. Actually, every human being can live without wickedness. We can live happily, but we need to love and honor each other. It's a mistake to think one is superior to others. If we meditate, we'll have proper consideration for others.

Devotee:

When I meditate, I become aware of consciousness in my body, but consciousness is all-pervasive. Does this mean that consciousness is only in living things?

BABA:

In Tapas you lose the smaller identity of ego. It's like this, when someone asks where you live, you answer in such and such a street or suburb. If you go to Sydney, you say you come from Perth. When you are overseas, you say you're from Australia. If you went to another planet, you would say you came from earth. In this way your consciousness expands and you identify with something much larger. Ultimately there is only one space.

There is a story about Adi Shankara for this. It is said that the Lord wanted to give Adi Shankara a lesson about ego. On his way to the Ganges, the Divine appeared before Adi Shankara in the form of a low caste 'untouchable' who was carrying home-made alcohol on his head, in a pot. "Go away!" shouted Adi Shankara. The untouchable replied, "Show me a place where either of us can go and still not continue to exist!" On hearing this, Adi Shankara prostrated to the man and said he considered him equal to his Guru.

Devotee:

Is God the sum total of consciousness or the master of consciousness?

BABA:

God is the one Supreme Consciousness that exists. All things come from God; all souls finally merge in God, like droplets of water merge into the ocean.

Devotee:

When I meditate there's a big fight within me at first. Part of my mind has a life of its own. Finally my inner mind goes to a certain place and I don't want to leave there! Can you comment on this?

BABA:

Yes, I understand. The mind is out of control and has acquired so many habits. This is the final struggle. The mind will have to find peace and tranquility. Don't brood over things or feel irritated. Be a valiant soldier. Keep going.

Devotee:

Does meditation cleanse the mind?

BABA:

Yes.

Devotee:

When meditating with you in October's programs, my meditations were very good and the time went so fast. Since then I have days when I feel like I have never meditated before in my life. Some days I can meditate peacefully and other days when I meditate, all my problems come into my thoughts and keep coming back like a record. How do you stop the attachment to your thoughts when meditating, especially when I get troubled thoughts?

BABA:

When troubling thoughts come in meditation, always remember that you are that Immortal Soul, beyond this physical body, and nothing can trouble or harm you. With polite firmness, ignore all thoughts and believe that Baba is always there with you.

Devotee:

Babaji, sometimes when I'm working very quickly, I find that the mind gets very excited. Is it because I'm working too quickly, or have I just not controlled the mind properly?

BABA:

You are not controlling the mind, and so it is getting involved too much into the tasks. With meditation, you will develop the ability to control the mind properly. Then you will be able to work very quickly, but keep the mind quiet and controlled.

Devotee:

Could You please speak about the use of mantras in spiritual exercises?

BABA:

Recitation of mantras is a preliminary exercise to help control the mind. They were composed by great Sages and have beautiful meanings. Reciting mantras can help to channel the emotional energies. When reciting the mantra, the mind should be focused there, and then this focusing of the mind will help to control it.

Devotee:

Can You please speak about reciting mantras while we are working, or while we are meditating?

BABA:

It is fine to recite the mantra while one is working, that is good. During meditation however, it is better if no mantra is recited at that time. It can be recited before the meditation, but not during the meditation. The aim of this technique of meditation is that the mind will not need a mantra to help it to quieten. The mind itself becomes quiet with this technique.

Devotee:

We hear of great souls such as Shivabalayogi and Ramana Maharshi, and others who simply attained Self-Realization directly. It seems as though, when the soul is ready, the Self- Realization simply happens. Does sadhana make us ready, or does it happen by itself?

BABA:

Yes, sadhana gets us ready. The self-effort, the sadhana—meaning efforts to achieve—is very important. Self-Realization occurs when the soul becomes ripe through sadhana.

Devotee:

In Advaita, it is said that all is One. If all is One, how does God get involved?

BABA:

God Himself does not get involved in the creation. He is perpetually in Mahasamadhi. The creation has happened because of God, but not according to any plan of God's. From Him, a spark called mind has come out, and this has given rise to the illusion of the individual.

Devotee:

Then why do we pray to God, if He doesn't get involved in the creation?

BABA:\

Mind's consciousness coming out of God is like the sun's ray coming out of the sun. Now, at present, the mind's consciousness is distracted, and thus fear and cravings develop. Through prayer, this distracted mind becomes more concentrated, and when the mind becomes concentrated, it turns inwards towards God. There is no third way for this mind's consciousness—it is either directed outwards towards the creation, or is turned inwards towards God. God does not have resolutions of the mind. Otherwise, we could ask Him why we have suffering. This world and creation has happened due to Him, but not by His wishes. Just like with a Yogi, he simply radiates his blessings to all around him. He does not direct the blessings to particular people.

Devotee:

So concentrating the mind means it will go back to God?

BABA:

Yes, concentration, without any resolution. If one has resolutions, then one becomes stuck on those resolutions. The mind must achieve mano laya, as it is called in spiritual terms. The mind must become quiet. If it is concentrated, then it becomes focused. If it is distracted, then it expands out into the world.

Devotee:

Could Baba please discuss the six shapes of the mind a little more?

BABA:

The ancient sages have seen that there are six different shapes that the mind can take. They named them as Kama (extreme greed), Krodha (extreme anger), Madha, (false pride), Lobha (stinginess), Moha (attraction to material things), Matsarya (jealousy). These are the six extreme shapes that the mind can take on. Of these, perhaps Matsarya is the most common.

Now in functioning in this world it might, for instance, be necessary in some situations to show a little anger. It may be necessary to achieve some outcome. But, if it is too much, then you will harm yourself and also those around you. So it is a matter that the mind should not take these on too much, unnecessarily and get totally caught up in them.

Devotee:

Why do we dream?

BABA:

Dreaming is a very peculiar state. There is no definite explanation for dreams, except that it is definitely an illusion within the mind. In a dream you can create a huge scene with many characters, and then suddenly when you get up you see that you're just dreaming. It may be from something simple like strong food just before going to sleep, so sages have recommended taking a small amount of light food. Or it may come from a strong resolution of the mind. The dreams themselves will vary so that some may be strong and appear very vivid and they stay in your mind when you awaken, while others may be weak and indistinct and difficult to recall later.

Devotee:

Could Baba please discuss physical pain? I have sometimes heard Baba say that the body itself is a disease.

BABA:

Yes, and sometimes I say it is a rare gem. But philosophically it can be seen that if you have a body, the consciousness then gets involved to become the mind and gets sucked into the world. There is no guarantee of the body remaining healthy at all times. It is inevitable to have some disease, if you have a body. So in the Mrityunjaya Mantra, *Om Triayumbakam Yajamahe Sugandhim Pustivardhanam Urvarukamevabandanam Mrityormokshiya Mamratat,* we pray: when the body finally drops by itself, then I— the imagined conscious self—merges with the Ultimate Truth that is Divine and gets liberated once for all; let me go back to God and do not have to get involved with any other physical body. Just like the pumpkin is ripe and opens by giving way and the seeds get liberated. However, as long as the physical body is there and can be kept as healthy as possible it is to be considered a rare gem. Through which we can withdraw our minds back into the Real Supreme Self.

OM TAT SAT

Glossary

A

Adharma—wrong behavior

Adi Para Shakti—first invisible energy

Advaita—philosophy of non-duality

Ahamkara—individuating principle (ego)

Ananda—bliss

Anantham—boundless

Arati—offering of light to the respected image of the divine

Arjuna—the devotee of Shri Krishna in the Bhagavad-Gita

Ashram—spiritual place of retreat

Aswamedha Yajna—a fire sacrifice for the purpose of gaining 'name and fame'

Atman—the Immortal Soul

Atma Vicharam—Self-Inquiry

B

Bhajans—devotional songs

Bhakti Marga (Bhakti Yoga)—the path of devotion

Bhava—the mind's feelings focused to a single-pointed intensity

Bhava Samadhi—state of devotional trance

Bhiksu—the one who receives alms; wandering monk

Bhikshana—alms

Bhrikuti—spot between the eyebrows; the focus-point during practice of Dhyana

Bhima—one of the Padhava brothers in the epic *Mahabharata*

Boons—blessings from the Divine

Brahmari Panayam—a breathing exercise

Brahman—the All-Pervading Divine

Brahma Vidya—knowledge of God

C

Crores—millions

D

Dakshina—devotional offering of wealth

Darshan—radiance of the Divine

Deeksha—initiation

Deva Loka—the realm of the gods

Devata—form of God; deity

Dharma—your duty; correct behavior

Dharmatma—righteous soul

Dholak—Indian drum

Drishya—the scene of the mind

Dhyana—single-pointed attention; meditation

Dvaita—duality

G

Gurukulam—Guru's spiritual institution

H

Hanuman—a hero of the epic *Ramayana* who aided Lord Rama in defeating the forces of demons

I

Ishtadeva—a devotees' chosen form of the Divine

J

Janaka—Shri Rama's father-in-law

Jnana—knowledge

Jnana Yoga—the path of Ultimate Knowledge

Jivanmukta—one who is liberated while still alive in the physical body

Jivatman—the limited self-identification; the small imagined self

K

Kali Yuga—the age of Kali

Kama—greed

Karma—action

Karma Rahasya—secret of karma

Karma Sadhana (Karma Yoga)—achievement of Yoga through service

Kauravas—Pandavas' cousins in epic *Mahabharata*

Krishna—God's incarnation who gave Bhagavad-Gita

Krodha—extreme anger

Kundalini—energy that is spread in the body

L

Leela—divine play

Lobha—extreme stinginess or meanness

M

Madha Ahankar—false pride; arrogance

Mahabharata—the story of Pandavas and Kauravas

Mahasamadhi—the supreme state of total mental stand-stillness, without any wavering

Mano Laya—receding of the mind; consciousness going back to the Self

Matsarya —jealousy

Moha—extreme attachment to the materialistic world

Moksha—final liberation

Mudras—spontaneous divine expressions with the hands

N

Namaskar—bowing with devotion

Narada—the celestial sage

Nirvikalpa Samadhi—complete absorption in the Self; beyond all experience

Nirodha—extinction

P

Pandavas—heroes of the epic *Mahabharata*

Pranayam—breathing exercises for mind control

Prarabdha Karma—action due to the acquired habits of the mind

Prasadam (Prasad)—blessed food

Puja—worship

R

Rama—hero of the epic *Ramayana*; incarnation of God

Ravana—the demon king defeated by Lord Rama in the epic *Ramayana*

S

Sadhak—spiritual aspirant

Sadhana—efforts to achieve pure mind

Sage—Saint

Sakshatkaram—direct realization of God

Samadhi—the state of absorption in the Self

Samskaras—acquired habits of the mind

Samsara—this world appearance

Sanyas—life of sacrifice

Sannyasi—monk

Sankalpa—mind's resolution

Sashtanga namaskaram—prostration symbolizing complete surrender

Satguru—the One True Guru

Satsang—company of the good and noble

Satvic—pure; righteous

Seenu—as Baba was affectionately known before Tapas

Seva—selfless service

Shakti—divine energy

Shanti—peace

Shivalingam—symbol of Lord Shiva

Sloka—verse of scripture

Sukha—peaceful bliss

T

Tapas—severe spiritual austerities of meditation for Self-Realization

Tapasya—purifying austerities

U

Unchavriti—a life of the highest virtue

Upadesham—ordainment; God's pre-ordainment

V

Vajrasana—sitting on your knees; the diamond posture

Vasanas—impressions of the mind's lust and greed

Veda Vyasa—the Great Sage who composed the epic *Mahabharata*

Vibhuti—sacred ash used for blessings

Videhamukti—liberation attained when the physical body is dropped

Viswarupa—God seen as the universe

Viyoga—away from its origin

Y

Yoga—reunion of the mind with its origin—the Ultimate Self

Yoga Sadhana—efforts which cultivate union of the mind

Yoga Vasistha—ancient scripture that recounts the dialogue between Lord Rama and his Guru Vasistha about the Ultimate Truth

Yogi—one who has abandoned all cravings of the mind and is settled effortlessly in the Ultimate Self and totally contented there

Yudhishthira —eldest brother of Pandavas in the epic *Mahabharata*

Contacts

**For all spiritual questions, please use this email address:
srby@gorge.net**

India

Sri Shivabalayogi Maharaj Trust (Ashram)
180-C Rajpur Rd,
Rajpur P.O., Dehradun- 248009, U.A. India
Tel: 91-135-2734214

USA

Shivabala-Shivarudrabalayogi Misssion (USA)
Charlie and Carol Hopkins
241 Cooper Avenue
Underwood, WA 98651 USA
Tel: 509-493-5209 E-mail: cah@gorge.net

Stephen Scheer
14956 NW Mill Road
Portland, OR 97231 USA
Tel: 503-285-6756 E-mail: scc17@aol.com

Australia

Shivabala-Shivarudrabalayogi Misssion (Australia)
Doris Brophy
Postal Address: 25 Truslove Way
Duncraig, Western Australia 6023, Australia.
Tel: (08) 9447-2126 E-mail: dorisb@iinet.net.au